# The Human Race To Destroy Planet Earth

## By

## Mayloemrojo El Bey

The Human Race To Destroy Planet Earth
ISBN 9781931671910
Library of Congress Control Number 2022942486
Copyright © 2022 by Mayloemrojo El Bey
Ma'at American Aborigine Tribal Nation
P.O. Box 10618
Casa Grande, AZ 85130

Printed in the United States of America. All rights reserved under International Copyright Law. Contents and/or cover may not be reproduced in whole or in part, in any form or by any means, without the express written consent of the Publisher.

Table of Contents

Synopsis ..................................................................... 4

Introduction .............................................................. 5

Chapter 1. Defining Competition and Commerce .......... 10

Chapter 2. Who Competes and Why .............................. 16

Chapter 3. The Desire to Compete: Nature or Nurture ... 43

Chapter 4. Survival of the Fittest: Was Darwin's Theory Correct? ......................................................... 59

Chapter 5. Effects of Competition and Commerce .......... 75

Chapter 6. Making The Universal Move To A Better Economy ....................................................... 84

Chapter 7. The Human Body: A More Effective Economic System ......................................... 123

Chapter 8. Our Resource-Based Solution: "MEET & GREET" ...................................................... 130

Chapter 9. Eliminating Our Worst Enemy: FEAR ........ 133

Conclusion ............................................................... 154

## Synopsis

It was Albert Einstein who once said, "The true definition of madness is repeating the same action, over and over, hoping for a different result." This book addresses the issues and gives viable solutions to the social ills of man brought on by an out dated and archaic monetary system that has led to wars, poverty, destruction, racism, elitism, and a competitive driving force that pervades every part of human life. This monetary system has left thousands of years of devastation in its wake, that can only be cured by its radical elimination and replacement by a resource-based economy, along with a radical change in man's mindset and values, lest he destroy himself and the planet he inhabits.

## Introduction

*Life is a competition not with others, but with ourselves. We should seek each day to live stronger, better, truer lives; each day to master some weakness of yesterday; each day to repair a mistake; each day to surpass ourselves.*
*- David B. Haight -*

Competition, which is an outgrowth of commerce, has and continues to destroy and devastate our world and the people. It is the culture of a patriarchal society to compete for everything from love to luxuries. It stems from pride, vanity, and egotism. A friend once told me, "It seems everybody wants to turn everything we enjoy into competition. We can't just cook; we have to see who's the best cook. We can't just play games; we have to see who is number one and give away medals for it."

The goal should always to be the best YOU can be. Somehow TV, movies, and marketing, have made us think we won't really know how good we are until we compete against and beat someone else. If it's speed, then why not time yourself and just beat the clock? Do you really need to see if you're faster than someone else?

I remember in the 9th Grade, I received the Gold Attendance award because for three years during that whole time I was the only student, among thousands, who was never late nor tardy. There had been two of us, but the other student was sick the day before the award ceremony, so they took his/her name off the list. How incredible! This, of course, was part of the military indoctrination of the public school system to prepare you later in life for slavery that they call employment.

I remember that I received the salutatorian award and was asked to deliver a short speech. My speech was about remembering and awarding the "under-dogs", those who were not usually recognized even though they too had gifts, talents, and contributions to make. I likened it to the game of tennis whereby, in those days, the winner jumped over the net and shook the hand of their opponent and congratulated him/her for a job well done.

I had always done well in school from the 3$^{rd}$ Grade on when a teacher encouraged me to write. I did well in Math, Science, and other subjects also. I thought it was because I tried harder since I was ostracized from classmates because I wore glasses, was skinny, and therefore quiet and shy. I loved reading magazines and books and spending time in the library. At the time, I had no idea that I had a high IQ. I never lauded anything over anyone else; I just enjoyed learning and creating things. However, I remember years later when I ran into an old classmate, she made fun of me by saying that I thought I was better than everyone else, but I ended up having to get a job like everyone else. I didn't understand her bitterness nor why she felt the way she did. From my understanding, wasn't getting a job the end goal anyway? I realized that teachers and others made people think I was going to be and do something so special. Yes, I had scholarships but I would learn later what a farce it all is.

Where does the competitive spirit come from? Are we born with it? Does society teach you to be this way? Is it an inherent survival of the fittest, like Darwin's theory proposes? Are we no better than the animals? Is the world just made up of winners and losers?

Competition appears to be war on a more non-life threatening level. Just think about all the games we play: Chess, Checkers, Card Games, Sports. We always have to keep score. We always have challengers. We're taught this behavior in our families, in school, and we carry it to our jobs, our social interactions, and in our relationships. And we wonder why there are so many dysfunctional families, unhappy and unfilled slaves (workers), abusive relationships, and divorces.

    We have been separated and divided. We do this to ourselves. It's okay to be a part of different sects, groups, and organizations. The problems arise when we start to compete with each other instead of working and networking together as a whole. Most of us don't really realize that we are a part of the whole, that we are each important and significant, that so are others, and that when we hurt and harm each other, we are also hurting and harming ourselves.

    However, through it all, the main culprit is the monetary system. It's not the form or the style. It's not that it would be better if it were run by communists, capitalists, or some other political ideology. It's the profit-seeking monetary system itself. There was a time when it was needed when our society was more primitive. Today, with all of our advancements and technology, it is no longer needed, and in fact, not only does it hinder our progress, it is the cause of 99% of all of the problems that exist.

    We'll examine and take a look at where this competitive spirit comes from and how the monetary system, which brings all of its mind-altering and stagnating values, plays a major part. Then, hopefully, we can entertain a viable solution to deter our own destruction and extinction as a species. Many have written on this subject. There are countless movies and videos that some of us have seen. However, when will man heed the voices crying in the wilderness? This book is my cry.

## Chapter 1. Defining Competition and Commerce

*Anybody can win unless there happens to be a second entry.*
*- George Ade -*

**Definition of Competition**

Webster's online dictionary defines competition as "1: the act or process of competing :RIVALRY: such as a: the effort of two of more parties acting independently to secure the business of a third party by offering the most favorable terms, e.g. contractors in competition for the contract to build the new school; b: active demand by two or more organisms or kinds of organisms for some environmental resources in short supply such as the Interspecies competition for food; 2: a contest between rivals such as in a gymnastics competition;
e.g. one's competitors' faced tough competition."

As such is typical of the English language, to further complicate matters, there is more definition. The definition of the word "compete" is "to strive consciously or unconsciously for an objective (such as position, profit, or a prize): be in a state of rivalry, competing teams, companies competing for customers." However, can anyone really compete unconsciously, that is, be unaware of what you are doing? To do something unconsciously means you have been conditioned or brainwashed whereby your actions are automatic without you realizing it consciously. This is what society has created. There is a built-in drive to compete for just about everything that exists. It's as if we have been trained to believe that "there is no such thing as a free lunch", and "you don't get something for nothing". We hear these statements all the time.

But let's ask ourselves, who is doing the giving and who is getting? Was not this earth and land here before one human being arrived here? Also, those same ones are not here today. Did any one of us ask to come into this existence? Who set up this system whereby we have to work and slave just to eat, live, and survive each day?

So, let's return to our definition. Let's look at the etymological definition, that is, the root or origin of the word. As we proceed, ask yourselves: which comes first, the act or the word(s) to describe it?

competition (n.)

c. 1600, "action of seeking or endeavoring to gain what another is endeavoring to gain at the same time," from Late Latin *competitionem* (nominative *competitio*) "rivalry," in classical Latin "agreement," noun of action from past participle stem of *competere* (see compete). Meaning "a contest for something, a trial of skill as a test of superiority or fitness" is from 1610s. Sense of "rivalry in the marketplace" attested from 1793; that of "entity or entities with which one competes" is from 1961, especially in business.

Entries linking to competition

compete (v.)

1610s, " to enter or be put in rivalry with," from French compéter "be in rivalry with" (14c.), or directly from Late Latin competere "strive in common, strive after something in company with or together," in classical Latin "to meet or come together; agree or coincide; to be qualified," from com "with, together" (see com-) + petere "to strive, seek, fall upon, rush at, attack" (from PIE root *pet- "to rush, to fly"). According to OED, rare 17c., revived from late 18c. in sense "to strive (alongside another) for the attainment of something" and regarded early 19c. in Britain as a Scottish or American word. Market sense is from 1840s (perhaps a back-formation from competition); athletics sense attested by 1857. Intransitive use is by 1974. Related: Competed; competing.

Using the same source, Webster's online dictionary, let's take a look at the brother of competition: commerce. The definition of commerce is described as:

1: social intercourse: interchange of ideas,
opinions, or sentiments... a negotiated peace
that will reestablish
intellectual commerce among them ...— P.
B. Rice
2: the exchange or buying and selling
of commodities on a large scale involving
transportation from place to place, a major
center of commerce, e.g.
interstate commerce

3: SEXUAL INTERCOURSE
archaic
: COMMUNE

Now, let's take a look at what the online etymology definition furnishes:

commerce (n.)

1530s, "social intercourse;" 1580s, "interchange of goods or property, trade," especially trade on a large scale by transportation between countries or different parts of the same country, from French commerce (14c.), from Latin *commercium* "trade, trafficking," from com "with, together" (see com-) + *merx* (genitive *mercis*) "merchandise" (see market (n.)). It also was the name of a card game very popular in 1770s and '80s. As a verb, "have dealings with," 1590s. Related: Commerced, commercing.

The most interesting part of all of this is the terms "social intercourse" and "sexual intercourse". It has been so ingrained in our society, that it makes you believe this is as normal as saying hello to a neighbor or having sex between two consenting adults. We've been doing it (no pun intended) for so long, we think it's just normal to buy and sell goods to each other and use a monetary system for which we all must compete to keep and maintain, or else for fear we won't be able to have all of the things we need, like the basics for survival, and the things we are made to think we want, thanks to marketing and advertising.

Due to those who have fooled us by creating a false sense of scarcity and fear, commerce and competition walk hand in hand like fraternal brothers - both resembling each other, existing within their own separate placenta, but born from the same systematic womb of capitalistic profit-seeking and self-preserving survival.
(Sources: https://www.etymonline.com; https://www.merriam-webster.com/dictionary)

## Chapter 2. Who Competes and Why

*Insecurity is at the heart of every rivalry.*
*- Beth Moore -*

  If no one paid us, if money were no issue and all the resources were available, there would be no need to hoard, no need to compete for resources, no need for crime, and no need for criminal laws to exist. The goal would be to sustain and maintain for the good of the family, the tribe, the community, the planet, and for the next generations to come. Resources would be utilized only when others like them are immediately replaced. For example, cut down a tree, plant another one. The emphasis would be away from more technology (machines) to mankind, just as Charlie Chaplin so lovingly and pleadingly urged us.

  With regard to space, most people crowd into one small area, either because they were born there, can't afford to live anywhere else, are afraid to venture anywhere else, or are there because commerce wills it (builds it). I cannot even count the number of times we have driven through state territory after territory and see empty homes and undeveloped land. I'm talking miles and miles. This is just in the Americas, known traditionally as the States of the

Union (United States). Although I have not as yet travelled abroad, thanks to the wonders of the Internet, I've seen a multitude of photos and videos and read articles and online content about other countries on the map. The social ills appear to be the same.

Everything begins and ends with the basic necessities to live. It was in college that I learned about Maslow's Hierarchy of Needs. Of course, Maslow, being a male, expressed these needs in terms of hierarchy or tier. It has been my experience that our needs as living beings is more a matter of cycles, that is, when you need certain things. This makes it more of a rounded or spiral rather than a hierarchy or tier. Also, along with what we need is why we need. What creates need? A real or perceived lack. In reality, we lack absolutely nothing. We are totally complete within ourselves and have all the resources available on this planet. It is a gift given to us the day we were created.

Just as a woman who realizes she is going to have a baby, prepares the external environment with all the necessities for her coming child, so did the universe prepare life on this planet for us. We have all the resources available to learn, discover, explore, and create. We are thinking and creative beings. Most people believe that if you didn't have a system where people have to go to work each day and the necessities of life were free, nothing would get built, that infrastructure, highways, and waste systems would never get put in place. This is completely absurd! Just think back, or better yet research, to the times when ancestors were settling new lands and venturing into new frontiers. No one paid them to build homes, roads, sewage system, wells, and waterways. They were families (tribes) using the free resources of the land to make sure they had food, water, and shelter.

As I write this, I'm reminded of one of the first episodes of the TV show *Bonanza*. The character, Ben Cartwright, portrayed by the late silver fox Lorne Green, stated that not one tree was cut down unless they planted another. He was expressing the give and take relationship that should exist between the people and the land of which they are given to use. Freely use and then give back to continue the cycle so that others may also do the same.

Along with food, water, and shelter, of course people also need clothing. The need for clothing has always been to protect against exposure to the elements and capture bodily excretions that require discreetness and privacy. Animals and other resources have usually served as a means for clothing. Although the ancestors killed buffalo, deer, lions, and wild boar for this purpose, they also served as food for them in most cases. Although I don't judge anyone for their survival choices, it would seem that I agree more with the use of sheep for clothing. Sheep do not need to be killed to use their wool. The sheep simply grow the wool back. It seems so much more economical and efficient and I'm sure it's a better preference for the sheep than the alternative left for other animals who are also eaten.

    Yes, it's true, as time moves forward, a great number of modern conveniences have been created. I think it's interesting that we file patents on inventions, claiming our intellectual property so we can either make money from the invention or sue (money damages) anyone who uses the patent to create something similar or wants to use the item without our authorization, usually for which we receive payment. What a great system for those who want to use these items. Therefore, we believe we have to have a medium of exchange or currency so we can handle these transactions. This would be fine in and of itself if it weren't for the fact that we have made commerce out of the basic necessities such as food, water, and shelter. Then we put regulations in place to make sure people are unable to acquire these items and provide for their families (tribes) unless they go to a job (slavery) and work for some company, who will give them paper in exchange, that they can then take to another company or individual to purchase what they need. We seem to think this is perfectly normal because we have been doing this for millennia. If this system is so normal and so great, why is there still rampant homelessness, poverty, hunger, and consequently crime?

It is clear that this is not how it was intended to be. So, before readers start formulating opinions that I am supporting communism, or any other kind of "ism", let me state that I believe in a different and more efficient type of exchange. It boils everything down to the basics. It's energy exchange for products and services. No living, breathing, thinking organism should go without food, water, shelter, or clothing. Each family (tribe) should have and be able to freely utilize the tools and resources needed to provide this. Some of the major problems:

- People believe they actually own things
- People don't comprehend that they are only caretakers

- People don't know why they here
- Systems of brainwashing and conditioning have been put in place to destroy the family unit

Have any of us taken time to think about why we're doing what we're doing and for what? We are so caught up in survival mode, fatigued from over work, exhausted from fighting traffic to find a job or get to and from a job, suffering anxiety from hearing about catastrophe after catastrophe, and confused by so much propaganda, we don't have or take time to sit down and think rationally and logically about what we are doing.

How can we possibly believe that we actually own anything? We were born naked from the womb. The only thing we can claim is our physical body, our spirit, and our soul. When we leave this planet, we won't even take our bodies with us. Even the body, we cannot claim because it was our parents (our ancestors) to whom we give credit for its pro-creation.

Everything we find here on this planet does in a sense belong to us, but not to own, to use for our good, for our purpose, to live and to share with those around us. No matter what you accumulate here, you can take nothing with you. Some of us even try to justify our horde and greed by saying we want to leave a legacy or inheritance for our progeny. This sounds good, but let's face it, our progeny has everything they need just as we do, that is, if we don't horde, stop killing each other, stop competing and taking from each other, and realize we are all a part of each other. Every one of us in on the same ship, planet Earth. If one part suffers, we all suffer.

    When we create something, we use, along with our gifts, talents, and abilities, the resources here on this planet. Since there is really nothing new under the Sun, we only re-vamp, change, revise, alter, or adjust what has already been, whether we are aware of it or not. Those who came before us had to create, using what was available to them during their time, that is, with the resources and discoveries of which they were aware. Others who came after them, benefited from their efforts. We all build upon the work of those who came before us. So, how can we say we actually own anything and claim that it is our intellectual property?

    It is man's ego, vanity, and selfishness, born out of a monetary system that has created a world of misplaced values and morals. Most of us don't realize that we were placed here as stewards, caretakers, and custodians of this planet. Everything is for our use, not to dominate and hoard everything here. It is humorous but at the same time disheartening to watch cartoon characters who depict real-life lunatics, who continually espouse how they want to "take over the world!"

This usually stems from those who don't really know why they are here and especially don't know who they are. There is a void inside of them that they try to fill with everything outside of themselves. They blame others, they blame God, and then reject others and reject that there is a Creator. Their deranged minds begin to believe that they are the God of everyone else, not understanding that the true God lives within them and within all others and that they are a part of each other. They don't realize that they are a micro version, that is, a hologram, of the macrocosm. They don't understand that they are immortal souls having a human experience.

Most of us don't realize that we have been brainwashed and conditioned to compete and believe this monetary system is the only way to live. We believe the world would somehow crumble if money, in whatever form, was no longer required just to live, eat, have shelter, and survive. Our minds cannot even fathom how it would be possible to survive without it. In fact, cognizant dissonance keeps some of us from even entertaining such a "ridiculous" thought. This cognizant dissonance occurs when new, rational, scientific or proven information is presented to a mind that cannot and will not accept anything that conflicts with its cherished and beloved, though usually non-rational, beliefs.

    We are products of what marketing and advertising, tools used to sustain this world of commerce and competition, tells us to believe, want, and even need. Our egos are stroked when we think of how much better off we are than those on the lower rung of the social class, and how much better off we are to live in this country (whatever country that may be) than our "enemies". Just think how absurd it would be for birds to think they are better than other birds, or any of the other species to do and think the way we do. Usually, one species does not devour and destroy their own. Humans, on the other hand, in our infinite wisdom, intelligence, and knowledge, kill, destroy, ostracize, rape, murder, torture, discriminate, compete, and divide ourselves. And we dare call ourselves the advanced species!

**Why do we compete?**

    Each of us would do well to study the elements in

the human body and compare them to the elements found in our environment. Just about every element on earth and in the atmosphere is found in the human body. This, of course, is referring to natural and pure elements, not those which are synthetic or man-made. Everything created is based on the model of the human body and its functions and structure. Again, as stated earlier, we are complete and have all that we need. So, why compete?

Are all games based on who can beat the opponent and declared the winner? Can we play them without keeping score and be satisfied with it? Will this be as much fun? This will take a mind reset from the patriarchal conditioning and brainwashing that has existed for millennia. Instead of values of winning and losing, how about one of learning and discovering your purpose? I propose a life filled with discovering yourself, your planet, your universe, then creating all things that either maintain life, extend life naturally, or make life enjoyable, then communicating and sharing your discovery with each other, without trying to use it to control, dominate, and bring commerce.

Are males innately competitive or does society (family dynamic) teach them to be so? Have most of us been conditioned to lose the joy of creating and only given to creating to patent and say it belongs to us for usage rights resell? This is the downfall of mankind. This has led to poverty, homelessness, discrimination, homicide and suicide, wars, divorce, breakdown in families (dysfunctional), and other such woes like slavery, being one of the biggest atrocities. Slavery still exists just in different forms such as employment and the prison system.

Lazy, control-hungry psychopaths are the culprits. Where did they come from? Are they our lower selves? Must they exist? Does Yin and Yang have to compete as in the Matrix when Neo had to battle Morpheus? Morpheus says he was preparing Neo to battle the enemy? When does it stop?

The Matriarch must rise up now and teach these boys how to behave and get along. They are destroying our world and themselves in the process. Some of them even know this. Their mindset is: "If I can't have it, no one will".

**Sibling Rivalry**

I think about the birth of my children – both from the same father, my ex-husband, both born in California, both living during a time when I had to work, had an okay-paying job, but still both are different. During both pregnancies, I took care of myself as best I could. I didn't even drink sodas, coffee, or eat sweets. I exercised and I walked every day. When each was born, I breastfed for 6 months. However, they were given a bottle of milk at night time to put them to sleep. My mother doted on both of them as at the time they were her first and only grandchildren. Even though my mother loved them both, it was obvious my mother preferred my son over my daughter, just like she preferred my brother over me. Because of this, I tried my best to treat my children the same or at least give them both all the love and acceptance equally that I could. There were many dynamics that made this most difficult: my ex-husband's substance abuse, my shortcomings as an imperfect human being and therefore an imperfect parent.

One major impact was the resentment and jealousy of my son with respect to my daughter. Because he was a baby and way too young in mind and development until about age 5, he doesn't remember how I loved him, cherished him and protected him. He doesn't remember all our special moments together. He was such a beautiful baby and energetic and happy as a child. He loved running and playing. My siblings and their consorts, as well as my ex-husband's family, all doted on him.

What he does remember is my daughter being born. Even though they are almost 2 years apart, he remembers how she invaded his world. No matter what I did, things changed. Now I had two little ones. The older had to help out sometimes with the younger. My ex-husband did not make my life easy which is part of a father's job. However, I relied on him most of the time to spend a lot of time with my son. It was my thought that a father could teach him to be a man; a father could show him and talk to him about things that I couldn't. So, even though I was the only one working most of the time, I felt my son was his responsibility while my daughter, being a girl, was mine. This, among many, was another mistake on my part.

It would have been fine if my ex-husband had been a responsible and reliable parent instead of an alcoholic, drug addict, and adulterer. I never really wanted to marry him but his Catholic mother and he pretty much took advantage of my sensibilities and weakness when I was 8 months pregnant with my daughter. I had this nagging feeling it was a mistake and I was right. I think it's ironic that the Doves of Happiness Chapel where we were married burned down two years later.

Because my ex-husband eventually was no longer there, and did not pay child support, which is one of the reasons he didn't come around, except to occasionally sleep with me, that eventually, I discontinued, my son and my daughter felt abandoned by him. They both dealt with it in their own ways. My daughter is very close to me and had always regarded my ex-husband like the baby dinosaur in the old TV show *Dinosaurs*. She looked at him as "not the mama". My son, on the other hand, took everything out on me. He resented me for having another child, for not being a perfect mother, for his father not being there, for not being wealthy, and for not being "White". To this day, he is still the same way, almost 40 years later. He doesn't talk to me or call me. He doesn't write to me and unfortunately, his children are the only grandchildren I have, so I don't get to see them or interact with them. Most of them are 18 or older, so they can make their own choices. They have chosen to do the same as my son.

Where there is no communication, there can be no reconciliation. My son knows this and prefers this. It takes this communication, along with forgiveness, openness, unconditional love, and a lot of patience to repair and even maintain any relationship. It also takes quiet meditation and introspection to discover our own limitations and weaknesses, to work on those faults, to really know ourselves, before we can connect with others.

    My son still feels jealousy toward my daughter, though he will never admit it. My daughter does not feel this jealousy toward him. She does not like his mistreatment of me, but she would be willing to forgive, forget, and move on, if he would openly admit to this lies and tell the truth. This is something he refuses to do. Like my mother who is no longer living, he is a narcissist also. He has allowed a false conception of competition to destroy one of what should be his most cherished relationships – that with his actual mother – one he will not truly realize how precious it is until it is too late.

    Too often this sibling rivalry is the scenario seen in many households; the rivalry even continues throughout adulthood. Many want to just blame the parents, especially the mother. However, each individual has access to healing these broken hearts. If they don't, they will never heal broken relationships and families. Hopefully, this book will, along with opening and exposing the wound, provide the needed ointment, sew up the severed ties, and allow time to provide the healing.

## Caste and Class Systems

<u>The Caste System</u>

The word "caste" can be traced to most Indian languages where the term "*jati*" is used for the system of hereditary social structures in South Asia. When Portuguese travelers to 16th-century India first encountered what appeared to them to be race-based social stratification, they used the Portuguese term "*casta*" — which means "race" — to describe what they saw. Today, the term "caste" is used to describe stratified societies based on hereditary groups not only in South Asia but throughout the world.

There are many who belong to what is called the Untouchable caste. They were assigned such tasks as making dung patties which are used for fuel and heat by members of all the castes. This job was considered so unclean that other castes did not associate with the members of society that performed it. Although born into the Kshatriya caste, Mahatma Gandhi spent much of his life working to bring the Untouchables equality. It was Gandhi who first named the Untouchables "Harijans," meaning "children of God."

If a Hindu person were asked to explain the nature

of the caste system, he or she might start to tell the story of Brahma — the four-headed, four-handed deity worshipped as the creator of the universe. According to an ancient text known as the Rigveda, the division of Indian society was based on Brahma's divine manifestation of four groups. It was from this design that Western Civilization created its caste system, which they call a class system. Supposedly, priests and teachers were cast from his mouth, rulers and warriors from his arms, merchants and traders from his thighs, and workers and peasants from his feet.

Others might present a biological explanation of India's stratification system, based on the notion that all living things inherit a particular set of qualities. Some inherit wisdom and intelligence, some get pride and passion, and others are stuck with less fortunate traits. Proponents of this theory attribute all aspects of one's lifestyle — social status, occupation, and even diet — to these inherent qualities and thus use them to explain the foundation of the caste system. Again, this is based on man's hierarchy, that is a patriarchal system.

There is an old fable that is told about an argument that the parts and organs of the body were having over which was the most important and essential. The hands argued that they make sure things get done and without them this would be impossible. The feet argued that they make the body mobile and no one could get anywhere, making them the most important and essential. In turn, the other parts followed suit, such as the heart saying if it didn't pump blood, the body would die; the lungs stating no air could get through so the body would die. Then the head spoke up emphatically insisted that it was the head and brains of the operation, that without its power of thought and thinking, the body would just remain a vegetable and therefore useless. The other parts had just about conceded until the bowels spoke up and said calmly that it was just as important. The other parts laughed and commented how absurd because it was the hidden, the lowest, and most disgusting, so how could it possibly be as important and essential as the rest of them. So the bowel closed up and refused to move. The hands were too weak to do anything, the feet didn't want to go anywhere, the heart felt faint, the lungs couldn't breathe very well. All of the organs were not operating well, in fact, the head started to ache so badly that it couldn't think. Finally, they all agreed that all the parts were equally important to a well and healthy functioning body.

## The Origins of the Caste System

According to one long-held theory about the origins of South Asia's caste system, Aryans from central Asia invaded South Asia and introduced the caste system as a means of controlling the local populations. The Aryans defined key roles in society, then assigned groups of people to them. Individuals were born into, worked, married, ate, and died within those groups. There was no social mobility.

There was an idea of an "Aryan" group of people that was not proposed until the 19th century. After identifying a language called Aryan from which Indo-European languages are descended, several European linguists claimed that the speakers of this language (named Aryans by the linguists) had come from the north — from Europe. Thus, according to this theory, European languages and cultures came first and were therefore superior to others. This idea was later widely promoted by Adolf Hitler in his attempts to assert the "racial superiority" of so-called light-skinned people from Europe over so-called dark-skinned people from the rest of the world — and thus provide justification for genocide. It is interesting to note that the so-called "elite" also hold and tout these same beliefs.

However, current research has thoroughly disproved this theory. Most scholars believe that there was no Aryan invasion from the north. In fact, some even believe that the Aryans — if they did exist — actually originated in South Asia and spread from there to Europe. Regardless of who the Aryans were or where they lived, it is generally agreed that they did not single-handedly create South Asia's caste system.

Therefore, it has been impossible to determine the exact origins of the caste system in South Asia. In the midst of the debate, only one thing is certain: South Asia's caste system has been around for several millennia and, until the second half of the 20th century, has changed very little during all of that time.

It can be seen that "race" is really a caste and social structure. It really has nothing to do with ethnic or cultural background. Actually, in the Western culture and now the rest of the world that has followed its lead, race has to do with the color of your skin, color of your eyes, your hair texture, etc.

Class vs. Caste

In ancient India, the ranked occupational groups were referred to as *varnas*, and the hereditary occupational groups within the *varnas* were known as *jatis*. Four *varna* categories were constructed to organize society along economic and occupational lines. Spiritual leaders and teachers were called Brahmins. Warriors and nobility were called Kshatriyas. Merchants and producers were called Vaishyas. Laborers were called Sudras.

In addition to the varnas, there is a fifth class in Hinduism. It encompassed outcasts who, literally, did all the dirty work. They were referred to as "untouchables" because they carried out the miserable tasks associated with disease and pollution, such as cleaning up after funerals, dealing with sewage, and working with animal skin.

Brahmins were considered the embodiment of purity, and untouchables the embodiment of pollution. Physical contact between the two groups was absolutely prohibited. Brahmins adhered so strongly to this rule that they felt obliged to bathe if even the shadow of an untouchable fell across them.

Some have argued that to immediately assume that ascribed social groups and rules prohibiting intermarriage among the groups signify the existence of a racist culture would be a false assumption. They insist that Varnas are not racial groups but rather classes. However, this is exactly the type of system that exists in America today. They call them classes. In theory this may be true, but in practice they operate the same as a caste system.

Even though the political and social force of the caste system has not disappeared completely, the Indian government has officially outlawed caste discrimination and made widespread reforms. This is due largely to the late great Mohandas Gandhi. Gandhi renamed the untouchables Harijans, which means "the people of God." Adopted in 1949, the Indian Constitution provided a legal framework for the emancipation of untouchables and for the equality of all citizens. In recent years, the Untouchables have become a politically active group and have adopted for themselves the name Dalits, which means "those who have been broken."

In America and other parts of the world that mimics its paradigm, there still exists widespread racial tension and problems. It seems man has always been obsessed with trying to think of himself as superior to those of his own species. Or, in the case of the "elite psychopaths", as a special and higher species. What is this disease within man that must prove he is better, special, or more superior than his own kind? Not all are like this or have this need for control. My only conclusion is that it stems from fear. Fear of his own true origins, fear of the truth about himself, fear that if he doesn't control others, they will eventually control him. (Source: https://www.ushistory.org/civ/8b.asp)

Differences Between Class and Caste Systems In Theory

According to Max Weber's definition, caste and class are both considered status groups. While castes are perceived as hereditary groups with a fixed ritual status, in theory, social classes are defined in terms of the relations of production. A social class is a category of people who have a similar socio-economic status in relation to other classes in the society. The individuals and families which are classified as part of the same social class are said to have similar life chances, prestige, style of life, attitudes etc.

In the caste system, status of a caste is determined not by the economic and the political privileges but by the ritualistic legitimation of authority. In the class system, ritual norms have no importance at all but power and wealth alone determine one's status. Take special note of the words "authority", "power" and "wealth".

Class system is said to differ in many respects from other forms of stratification—slavery, estate and caste system. There are textbooks written by MacIver, Davis and Bottomore where, in their observation, they consider caste and class to be polar opposites, that is antithetical to each other. According to the authors, 'class' represents a 'democratic society' having equality of opportunity, while 'caste' is obverse of it. This sounds good in theory.

In theory, the following are the main differences between class and caste systems:

1. Castes are found in Indian sub-continent only, especially in India, while classes are found almost everywhere. Classes are especially the characteristic of industrial societies of Europe and America. According to Dumont and Leach, caste is a unique phenomenon found only in India.

2. Classes depend mainly on economic differences between groupings of individuals—inequalities in possession and control of material resources—whereas in caste system non-economic factors such as influence of religion [theory of karma, rebirth and ritual (purity-pollution)] are most important.

3. Unlike castes or other types of strata, classes are not established by legal or religious provisions; membership is not based on inherited position as

specified either legally or by custom. On the other hand, the membership is inherited in the caste system.

4. Class system is typically more fluid than the caste system or the other types of stratification and the boundaries between classes are never clear-cut. Caste system is static whereas the class system is dynamic.

5. In the class system, there are no formal restrictions on inter-dining and inter-marriage between people from different classes as is found in the caste system. Endogamy is the essence of caste system which is perpetuating it.

6. Social classes are based on the principle of achievement, i.e., on one's own efforts, not simply given at birth as is common in the caste system and other types of stratification system. As such social mobility (movement upwards and downwards) is much more common in the class structure than in the caste system or in other types. In the caste system, individual mobility from one caste to another is impossible.

This is why, castes are known as closed classes

(D.N. Majumdar). It is a closed system of stratification in which almost all sons end up in precisely the same stratum their fathers occupied. The system of stratification in which there is high rate of upward mobility, such as that in the Britain and United States is known as open class system. The view that castes are closed classes is not accepted by M.N. Srinivas (1962) and Andre Beteille (1965).

7. In the caste system and in other types of stratification system, inequalities are expressed primarily in personal relationships of duty or obligation—between lower- and higher-caste individuals, between serf and lord, between slave and master. On the other hand, the nature of class system is impersonal. Class system operates mainly through large-scale connections of an impersonal kind.

8. Caste system is characterized by 'cumulative inequality' but class system is characterized by 'dispersed inequality.'

9. Caste system is an organic system but class has a [segment characteristic] where various segments are motivated by competition (Leach, 1960).

10. Caste works as an active political force in a village (Beteille, 1966) but class does not work so.

The question to ask is why are either caste or class needed in the first place? Why does there always have to be inequalities? Most of this stems from commerce that further enforces the drive to compete. Man, in his mind and thinking is still a primitive creature. He has utilized technology to create so many systems and designs and conveniences for himself, that is those who are not still fighting for the basic needs to live, and can afford all the technological luxuries. However, man still does not know himself, nor does he know how to control himself. He studies, studies, and studies, but never "able to come into the knowledge of truth".

(Source: https://www.yourarticlelibrary.com/sociology/differences-between-class-and-caste-systems/35101)

## Chapter 3. The Desire to Compete: Nature or Nurture

*A creative man is motivated by the desire to achieve, not by the desire to beat others.*
- Ayn Rand -

When we think of all the problems that exist, we simplistically conclude that there is something wrong with people. While this is true in some respect, these problems are merely symptoms of a bigger problem. People are reacting to the environmental system put upon them.

What makes men so competitive? Are they born with this? Freud seems to believe it is inherent in men to compete with their fathers for their mother's attention. It appears that men have this innate feeling that everything is an extension of themselves, actually just one part of themselves: phallic. You see this in everything they create: They make high rise buildings, steeples, products for use – such as bottles, etc. – mostly everything is shaped like a phallic. It's as if they are trying to overcompensate for feeling of inadequacy, feelings of manhood, feelings of control – by creating these shapes.

The hierarchal system, the pyramid – the low point where all the common people are – rising ever upward to the peak point, climaxing into the elite, the highest power.

The higher you go, the more thrill and the more you feel you've achieved. You are officially better than everyone else. "King of the Mountain" so to speak. That is, until some other "king" knocks you off and you go plummeting to your demise.

Women, who by nature are nurturers, have been taught as a result of capitalistic survival, to participate in these insane rituals. There are many books written to this effect.

According to Marilynne Robinson, author of "Competition", published in *Salmagundi* in 2005, Americans are told that we love competition, that we accept this without questioning the truth of the statement or even the meaning of the words. Even though we live in a diverse ethnic and religious society today, this "does not serve as a marker of nationhood". The author states that "a near approach to homogeneity seems to inflame ferocious antagonism against those who, as it were, cross themselves with too many fingers, or too few". This again pinpoints one of the biggest fears that exist today. We fear those whose ways and means differ from our own.

In fact, it is true that most of us do not really know much about other countries except what we read in books, magazines, the Internet, or so-called "news" that is full of propaganda and slanted to make the United States seems like angels and all others devils and terrorists. According to Robinson, this is what "fuels the force of competition", and because of this, we "can always be persuaded that any other country or region is a potential competitor", that is "a threat".

What is interesting of note is that Robinson states, "Oddly, though we admire the Europeans" and "do not compete with them". However, we do feel threatened by countries such as Japan who we believe are our "supposed competition" because of their "emerging economies". Robinson notes that there is "nothing healthy about seeing another country's prosperity as a competitive challenge to be dealt with". Of course the word for this is xenophobia. Robinson goes on to state that although it is the "brute masses" who can be blamed for these type of anxieties, it is "the narrative that produces the anxieties is the work of the elite". Also, it should be noted that it was the work of the carefully planned disastrous and inhumane self-inflicted 9-11 tragedy that was effected to cause fear and anxiety in the people so that we would perceive a specific country of other people as threats to our own welfare.

Robinson is correct that once we saw Japan as a super race. Today, things have changed and the Unites States is viewed as the super race and now begins to "cast about for new competitors" and that now "China has begun to haunt our dreams, and so has India". This preoccupation of our society with such matters that do not actually move us forward as a people. According to Robinson, "Either the great sullen bulk of the country is in the thrall of religious bigotry and tawdry consumerism, or the great, sullen bulk of the country has been corrupted by anti-religious bigotry and tawdry consumerism". She notes that competition "had an oddly elevated moral status derived ultimately from Social Darwinism", and that it is "a struggle for survival against anyone who can pose any kind of threat, actual or potential, or even imagined". She adds that poverty is a great asset in this competition in which the world is involved. Because of this, it is "improbable indeed that governments will work to raise the living standards or the expectations of their own people". She goes on to state that:

> *Toxic trash is shipped off to exotic lands to be picked apart by women and children for reuse, cheapening even more the electronic gimmicks we so enjoy. If one were to ponder the true cost of a thing in*

> *terms of what has really gone into the making of it – in terms, that is, of political cynicism, of cultural and environmental destruction and degradation, and of diminished health and life, with the consequences of all these things for subsequent generations, then it would be clear that we are subsidized by the desperation of the world's poor, present, and future. The implications of the current ethos of competition is that we must and should meet them on their own grounds. By creating an equivalent desperation among our own? So that we can do what? Impoverish these poor even further? To ask an archaic question, what good is being served?*

Robinson identifies competition as "the rationalizing influence in economic relations and argues that "capital has no loyalty except to profitability". Every day we "see the looting of those more or less attenuated communities we call companies – a word which means, at its root, people who break bread together." Robinson further states that "Towns and families are deprived and the satisfaction of livelihood are destroyed, with profitability or the interests of stockholders as pretext, or with the pleasures of the global market as excuse".

She notes that competition "has a sort of nationalist

sound, as if we were being asked to hold up our side, and as if, competition successfully completed, an anthem might be played, medals bestowed". However, she states, "But in fact the word is invoked in a new, radically non-national context. Work quietly and cheaply or your job will go to China. No one wants to know that you've served in the military, that you're a volunteer fireman, that you play blue grass guitar. Norman Rockwell is dead". We seem to feel there is "always some new peril" and that there is a "tension, a sense that something drastic or infernal could befall us, which has become so established in our thinking... as to have diminished our capacity for reasonableness and even for civilized aspiration".

According to Robinson, the "most destructive thing about competition as it is thought of and practiced now is that it is brutally indifferent in the particularity of culture and community". She says that it takes the word beyond politics by taking the decisions that reflect choices and values out of the hands of any specific population. Robinson concludes that because of this, "we cannot raise their minimum wage or provide maternity leave because it would raise the cost of labor, and therefore reduce our competitiveness in the global market".

[Source: *Salmagundi*, Fall 2005 - Winter 2006, No. 148/149 (Fall 2005 - Winter 2006), pp. 3-15, Published by: Skidmore College. https://www.jstor.org/stable/40549718]

Although Robinson hits the nail on the head, I would go further and say that it is commercialism in and of itself that brings about these woes and anxieties on the people due to the competition that fuels the entire process. We are so busy competing that we have forgotten about living.

In an article entitled "Competition and Feminism: Conflicts for Academic Women", by Evelyn Fox Keller and Helen Moglen, published in 1987 by The University of Chicago Press, the authors examine the roles of women with respect to their competition with each. Some of the highlights from their study:

> *The roles that we had played with one another: the too-good mother, the never-grateful-enough daughter, rivalry of loving sisters. We faced the ways in which we have competed as teachers, scholars, colleagues, friends, mothers, women.*
>
> *But as the doors to the ivory tower have swung open, as positions of influence and power have become available to women, we have lost both innocence and purity.*

> *We must recognize that competition creates special problems for women, for feminists most of all. The fact that women seem to experience different, deeper, and more painful forms of competition with one another than they do with their male peers.*
>
> *As colleagues have repeatedly told us, "We compare ourselves with women, not with men". "The success of men doesn't threaten me, but the success of women does". "Men can take it. They really ask for it because they already have so much". "Competition with women gets close to things that are really very scar[y]".*
>
> *Sometimes we are mothers, sometimes daughters, sometimes lovers, sometimes friends – and each of these roles is also split into good and bad. None of these relationships can be cleansed of the threatening feelings of envy and resentment – even of the aggression – that we associate with competition and have tried so hard and for so long to banish from our images of ourselves.*

I ask, why is this so? Is this innate or due to external conditioning? The authors also state that relationships between real sisters are frequently very close, which fosters considerable mutual dependency and deep love. But that those relationships also foster intense antagonisms to the point that the success of a sister is often equated with the failure of oneself. The authors state that "envy (and their intense discomfort with it) seem to be the emotion talked about with the most urgency by the women with whom we have spoken." It is this primary, they say, that makes competition with women so much more acute and painful that competition with men.

According to the study, sibling rivalry is based on a "model of siblings as well demarcated individuals, competing for the love of a mother – or father – which itself is assumed to be a scarce resource". The authors go on to say that frequently it seems that it is not the mother's love that is competed for but the mother herself. So that when one attempts to trace envy between siblings "(perhaps, given the intensity of the mother-daughter bond, the envy especially between sisters) to the quest for a mother's love, it is almost as if that love (whatever its quantity) is viewed by the daughter as capable of only supporting the life of one daughter." Therefore, in this case, "rivalry can feel deadly indeed".

An example is from a movie called *Black Swan*. The desire to compete and win above all else was so great and intense that the lead character saw everyone and everything as her competition – even the other side of herself (The White Swan). She was unable to see herself as both and ended up stabbing herself to death because she was threatened by her the mirror image and saw it as the competition.

The authors note that the very closeness of the sibling relationship seems to compel comparison of the partners – a comparison that can produce severe narcissistic injury when it reflects badly on oneself and, conversely, particular narcissistic pleasure when it reflects well. Instead of promoting the ease of sharing pleasure in each other's success, the very closeness of the sister-sister relationship appears under certain circumstances to "exacerbate the tendency to equate the other's success with one's own failure, and vice versa". According to the authors, there is a fear of abandonment provoked by unequal success in a relationship of strong mutual dependency, and that this can be seem even more so between best friends than sisters. These insecurities "devolve around the threat to sisterly bonding posed by the need or desire for external resources and rewards".

In two of the studies, the accounts are notable for the degree to which the focus is entirely on the avoidance of competition, the underlying assumption being that competition, conflict, and envy can be avoided. If only we are "good enough". The complex psychological roots of competition are not recognized, and conflict is seen as originating entirely from external sources. The presumption is that, "in a world of infinite resources, love and cooperation will prevail". The authors appear to disagree with this assumption.

In the third and fourth studies, the authors note that both of the stories appear to corroborate the view that competition increases with the magnitude of the stakes – that it is not so much poverty that creates the breeding ground for competition as it is the possibility of wealth. They also note that there is competition for nonmaterial stakes, such as power, influence, or love, and that there "are real differences emerging in our goals, values, and strategies that can never be resolved or banished".

The authors add that with the advent of status and power, women have begun to exhibit the kinds of behavior previously thought of as male but perhaps with a difference. The "dream of harmonious sisterhood" has not vanished but neither has it "softened the edge of sisterly rivalry when conflict and competition do erupt". Indeed, in some ways, it seems to make it worse. The authors state,

"Competition denied in principle, but unavoidable in practice, surfaces in forms that may be far more wounding, and perhaps even fiercer and more destructive, than competition, that is ideologically sanctioned". The authors reason that "conversely, the equation between conflict and competition lends all differences in goals and values the subjective character of a life and death struggle".

The authors state in their conclusion that in the prevailing, non-feminist view of human nature and the world that dominates organizational, economic, and evolutionary thought, individuals are assumed to be essentially autonomous units and the world "a finite reservoir of non-expandable and accordingly scare sources". In the struggle for survival that inevitably ensues, in which each individual is "primarily motivated by self-interest, competition (either tacit or overt) is obligatory". Indeed, so entrenched in this view of animate and inanimate nature that, in "most of the economic and biological literature, scarcity has come to be effectively synonymous with competition". In such a view, it is "cooperation that is seen as anomalous, as the problem in need of explanation". However, because we "are not atomistic individuals but fundamentally relational beings, self can never be totally separated by 'other', and cannot always draw the line between self-interest and altruism". Also, since resources are not fixed, "predetermined givens but are in fact functions of human need and ingenuity."

The authors note that institutional structures help to shape our interactions, as do our own expectations. The equation of one's success with another's failure is not only "an expression of bad faith, it is a stance that compels competition". Conversely, the commitment to the view that "what goes around, comes around" may be an unrealistic expression of good faith but, insofar as "such faith fosters cooperation and mutual responsibility, it is a commitment with real consequences". It provides an important catalyst to the kinds of efforts that can and do promote an expansion of existing resources.

Lastly, the authors note that however formative our family experiences, our relationships as colleagues are not, in fact, those of mothers and daughters or of sisters. Short of resolving residual conflicts in the domestic arena and reforming our expectations as mothers, daughters, and sisters, we can "at the very least recognize the inappropriateness of those expectations of each other as colleagues in a world beyond the family".

(Source: *Signs*, Spring, 1987, Vol. 12, No. 3 (Spring, 1987), pp. 493-511, Published by: The University of Chicago Press, https://www.jstor.org/stable/3174334)

Another example of "deadly competition" is from the TV Series *Hell's Kitchen*. I believe it was Season 12, Episode 10-11, where contestant Jessica Vogel, born October 18, 1983, begged Chef Gordon Ramsey to please, please let her stay and not be eliminated from the cooking competition. Apparently, sentiment is no place for a cooking competition with high sizzling "steaks" (stakes). Therefore, Jessica's plea went unheeded. A year later, Jessica died on July 30, 2018 from ulcerative colitis. She was an amazing chef. Instead of continuing to use her creative and wonderful gift for gourmet cooking, she suffered from hurt, dread, dejection, and humiliation.

**Who are our enemies?**

It's interesting how many people say they want world peace. It's as if it's the good moral sentiment to spout, but few not only do nothing to achieve it, most don't have a clue how to go about it. World peace takes "people peace", not only outside of themselves, but they must first look inwardly. It takes close, hard introspection to bring about knowledge of self, and in-tuning with one's higher self.

There are so many distractions and monetary goals of commerce and control by the elite that are geared to make sure you don't attain this level of peace and quiet, let alone attain satisfaction with yourself, your life, and the people around you. There is a constant screaming message (subliminal or otherwise) that you're not good enough or you don't have enough, that is, unless you buy the product that is currently being advertised and/or marketed.

We are made to think that the majority of the people around us are the enemy. We are made to feel afraid of anything different than us, especially if they come from a different region. We are made to be afraid of an invisible virus and think wearing masks and staying 6 feet away will protect us. Those tactics have been ingrained and indoctrinated in us for centuries, even millennia. However, as we have seen, these tactics come and go and are replaced by others.

I watched a few episodes of a TV series called *Cults and Extreme Beliefs*. It's interesting how they depicted specific religious beliefs such as Faith International, United Nation of Islam (not same as Nation of Islam), Jehovah Witnesses, and Federation of Latter Day Saints, as cults.

However, we could also say the same for Catholicism, Christianity, or any other religion. We could also include political groups such as Democrats and Republicans and even specific organizations. We could also include the elite and controlling government and its entities. If it's a matter of mind-control, coercion, manipulation, pedophilia, and abuse, it is a fact that it exists everywhere. Those who we are supposed to be able to trust and protect us, are just as guilty. Does this include all of them? Absolutely not. Fortunately, there are many exceptions.

    I know that I am a living, breathing, thinking and self-aware organism. I am made up of billions of cells that exist and are a part of organs and tissues. As a whole, I rarely think about each tiny cell. Sometimes when there is pain or dis-ease in an area of my body needing attention, I will then think about it in terms of doing what is needed to solve the problem, whether it is needed to stop doing something, apply something, ingest something, or expel something. Ironically, such is the case at the time I am writing these words. However, my cells do not compete with each other; they assist each other to make sure the body gets what it needs. We would do well to do likewise.

## Chapter 4. Survival of the Fittest: Was Darwin's Theory Correct?

*Seven social sins: politics without principles, wealth without work, pleasure without conscience, knowledge without character, commerce without morality, science without humanity, and worship without sacrifice.*
*- Mahatma Gandhi -*

Man did not evolve from lower life forms as we are given to understand the theory of evolution from Darwin. The Great Consciousness created all that there is, starting with other smaller forms of life. It would be from these patterns that the other life forms were created. Man was created and endowed with everything inside of him that comes from this planet. He is complete within himself. However, he, through technology, started destroying his environment for the sake of his created commerce. He will allow, once again, his discoveries and innovations to destroy him, if gone completely unchecked. There is a balance of natural law that must always be maintained. This includes Ying and Yang or just plain old give and take. This world was created with a symbiotic and synergistic model. Man has disrupted that structure and, if left unchecked, will destroy this planet and his human existence in the process. We must not allow the madness of the controlling few who call themselves "government" to continue with these same life-threatening tactics.

I began my college journey with a four-year scholarship to the University of Southern California (USC) to study Biomedical Engineering. The entire class except for me was made up of young, white males. The Director of the program, who was also one of the engineering course instructors, told me that I "didn't belong in that class". My first mistake was that I believed him. However, at the time I didn't understand it. Today, almost 50 years later, I have more knowledge and experience.

This occurred in 1974. Little did I realize then that due to my gender and ethnic background, I was not a wanted commodity in their Secret Society of elite sociopaths. They did not want me privy to the diabolical plans they had for the planet with regard to their New World Order.

So from where does this "I'm elite, special, privileged, and better than everyone else" state of mind come? Is man, or some of mankind, born with this mindset? Are they the "fittest" of the species (or elite and different species as some claim) and worthy of survival as opposed to the rest of us? Let's take a look at where some of this mindset originated. Below, for consideration is an article taken from: https://www.livescience.com/474-controversy-evolution-works.html. See if you agree.

## Was Darwin's Theory Correct?

*The Theory of Evolution by natural selection was first formulated in Charles Darwin's book "On the Origin of Species" published in 1859. In his book, Darwin describes how organisms evolve over generations through the inheritance of physical or behavioral traits, as National Geographic explains. The theory starts with the premise that within a population, there is variation in traits, such as beak shape in one of the Galapagos finches Darwin studied.*

*According to the theory, individuals with traits that enable them to adapt to their environments will help them survive and have more offspring, which will inherit those traits. Individuals with less adaptive traits will less frequently survive to pass them on. Over time, the traits that enable species to survive and reproduce will become more frequent in the population and the population will change, or evolve, according to BioMed Central. Through natural selection, Darwin suggested, genetically diverse species could arise from a common ancestor.*

*Darwin did not know the mechanism by which traits were passed on, according to*

*National Geographic. He did not know about genetics, the mechanism by which genes encode for certain traits and those traits are passed from one generation to the next. He also did not know about genetic mutation, which is the source of natural variation. But future research by geneticists provided the mechanism and additional evidence for evolution by natural selection.*

*But when given enough time and accumulated changes, natural selection can create entirely new species, a process known as "macroevolution," according to Derek Turner and Joyce C. Havstad in "The Philosophy of Macroevolution." This long-term process is what turned dinosaurs into birds, amphibious mammals (such as an animal called Indohyus) into whales and a common ancestor of apes and humans into the people, chimps and gorillas we know today.*

*Darwin also described a form of natural selection that depends on an organism's success at attracting a mate — a process known as sexual selection, according to Nature Education. The colorful plumage of peacocks and the antlers of male deer are both examples of traits that evolved under this type of selection.*

*How Did Whales Evolve?*

*One of the best examples scientists have of natural selection, is the evolution of whales. By using Darwin's theory as a guide, and understanding how natural selection works, biologists determined that the transition of early whales from land to water occurred in a series of predictable steps.*

*The evolution of the blowhole, for example, might have started with random genetic changes that resulted in at least one whale having its nostrils farther back on its head, according to Phys.org.*

*The whales with this adaptation would have been better suited to a marine lifestyle, since they would not have had to completely surface to breathe. Such individuals were more successful and had more offspring. In later generations, more genetic changes occurred, moving the nose farther back on the head.*

*Other body parts of early whales also changed. Front legs became flippers. Back legs disappeared. Their bodies became more streamlined, and they developed tail flukes to better propel themselves through water, according to the Natural History Museum.*

*Even though scientists could predict what early whales should look like, for a long time they lacked the fossil evidence to back up their claim. Creationists viewed this absence, not just with regard to whale evolution but more generally, as proof that evolution didn't occur, as pointed out in a Scientific American article.*

*However, since the early 1990s, scientists have found evidence from paleontology, developmental biology and genetics to support the idea that whales evolved from land mammals. These same lines of evidence support the theory of evolution as a whole.*

*In the first edition of "On the Origin of Species," Darwin speculated about how natural selection could cause a land mammal to turn into a whale. As a hypothetical example, Darwin used North American black bears (Ursus americanus), which were known to catch insects by swimming in the water with their mouths open, according to the Darwin Correspondence Project. "I can see no difficulty in a race of bears being rendered, by natural selection, more aquatic in their structure and habits, with larger and larger mouths, till a creature was produced as monstrous as a whale," he speculated.*

*The idea didn't go over very well with the public or with other scientists. Darwin was so embarrassed by the ridicule he received that the swimming-bear passage was removed from later editions of the book. Scientists now know that Darwin had the right idea but the wrong animal. Instead of looking at bears, he should have been looking at cows and hippopotamuses.*

*Other Theories of Evolution*

*Darwin wasn't the first or only scientist to develop a theory of evolution. Around the same time as Darwin, British biologist Alfred Russel Wallace independently came up with the theory of evolution by natural selection, according to the Natural History Museum. However, this had little impact.*

*"The concept of evolution as a historical event was a hot topic among biologists and geologists prior to Darwin's book because there was so much evidence accumulating, but I suspect biological evolution hadn't really impinged on people outside of the academic bunker," Dr. P John D. Lambshead, a retired science research leader in marine biodiversity, ecology, and evolution at The Natural History Museum, London, told All About History Magazine. "As long as science knew of no mechanism to explain how evolution happened it could be safely dismissed as a crank idea."*

*Meanwhile, French biologist Jean-Baptiste Lamarck proposed that an organism could pass on traits to its offspring, though he was wrong about some of the details, according to the University of California's Museum of Paleontology.*

*Like Darwin, Lamarck believed that organisms adapted to their environments and passed on those adaptations. He thought organisms did this by changing their behavior and, therefore, their bodies — like an athlete working out and getting buff —*

*and that those changes were passed on to offspring.*

*For example, Lamarck thought that giraffes originally had shorter necks but that, as trees around them grew taller, they stretched their necks to reach the tasty leaves and their offspring gradually evolved longer and longer necks. Lamarck also believed that life was somehow driven to evolve through the generations from simple to more complex forms, according to Understanding Evolution, an educational resource from the University of California Museum of Paleontology.*

*Though Darwin wasn't sure of the mechanism by which traits were passed on, he did not believe that evolution necessarily moved toward greater complexity, according to Understanding Evolution — rather, he believed that complexity arose through natural selection.*

*A Darwinian view of giraffe evolution, according to Quanta Magazine, would be that giraffes had natural variation in their neck lengths, and that those with longer necks were better able to survive and reproduce in environments full of tall trees, so that subsequent generations had more and more long-necked giraffes.*

*The main difference between the Lamarckian and Darwinian ideas of giraffe evolution is that there's nothing in the Darwinian explanation about giraffes stretching their necks and passing on an acquired characteristic.*

*What Is Modern Evolutionary Synthesis?*

*According to Pobiner, Darwin did not know anything about genetics. "He observed the pattern of evolution, but he didn't really know about the mechanism," she said. That came later, with the discovery of how genes encode different biological or behavioral traits, and how genes are passed down from parents to offspring. The incorporation of genetics into Darwin's theory is known as "modern evolutionary synthesis."*

*The physical and behavioral changes that make natural selection possible happen at the level of DNA and genes within the gametes, the sperm or egg cells through which parents pass on genetic material to their offspring. Such changes are called mutations. "Mutations are basically the raw material on which evolution acts," Pobiner said.*

*Mutations can be caused by random errors in DNA replication or repair, or by chemical or radiation damage, according to Nature Education. Usually, mutations are either harmful or neutral, but in rare instances, a mutation might prove beneficial to the organism. If so, it will become more prevalent in the next generation and spread throughout the population.*

*In this way, natural selection guides*

*the evolutionary process, preserving and adding up the beneficial mutations and rejecting the bad ones. "Mutations are random, but selection for them is not random," Pobiner said.*

*But natural selection isn't the only mechanism by which organisms evolve, she said. For example, genes can be transferred from one population to another when organisms migrate or immigrate — a process known as gene flow. And the frequency of certain genes can also change at random, which is called genetic drift.*

*The reason Lamarck's theory of evolution is generally wrong is that acquired characteristics don't affect the DNA of sperm and eggs. A giraffe's gametes, for example, aren't affected by whether it stretches its neck; they simply reflect the genes the giraffe inherited from its parents. But as Quanta reported, some aspects of evolution are Lamarckian.*

*For example, a Swedish study published in 2002 in the European Journal of Human Genetics found that the grandchildren of men who starved as children during a famine passed on better cardiovascular health to their grandchildren.*

*Researchers hypothesize that although experiences such as food deprivation don't change the DNA sequences in the gametes, they may result in external modifications to DNA that turn*

*genes "on" or "off."*
*Such changes, called epigenetic changes, do not modify the actual DNA sequence itself. For instance, a chemical modification called methylation can affect which genes are turned on or off. Such epigenetic changes can be passed down to offspring. In this way, a person's experiences could affect the DNA he or she passes down, analogous to the way Lamarck thought a giraffe craning its neck would affect the neck length of its offspring.*

*What Is The Evidence For Evolution?*

*The Theory of Evolution is one of the best-substantiated theories in the history of science. It is supported by evidence from a wide variety of scientific disciplines, including genetics, which shows that different species have similarities in their DNA.*
*There is also evidence supporting the Theory of Evolution in paleontology and geology. This is through the fossil record, which shows how that species that existed in the past are different from those present today, according to Bruce S. Lieberman and Roger L. Kaesler in "Prehistoric Life: Evolution and the Fossil Record" (Wiley, 2010).*
*There is also evidence for Darwin's theory found in developmental biology. It has been discovered that species that seem*

*very different as adults pass through similar stages of embryological development, suggesting a shared evolutionary past, according to the open-access textbook "Concepts of Biology."*

*The critical piece of evidence was discovered in 1994, when paleontologists found the fossilized remains of Ambulocetus natans, which means "swimming-walking whale," according to a 2009 review published in the journal Evolution: Education and Outreach. Its forelimbs had fingers and small hooves, but its hind feet were enormous relative to its size. The animal was clearly adapted for swimming, but it was also capable of moving clumsily on land, much like a seal.*

*When it swam, the ancient creature moved like an otter, pushing back with its hind feet and undulating its spine and tail.*

*Modern whales propel themselves through the water with powerful beats of their horizontal tail flukes, but A. natans still had a whip-like tail and had to use its legs to provide most of the propulsive force needed to move through water.*

*In recent years, more and more of these transitional species, or "missing links," have been discovered, lending further support to Darwin's theory. For example, in 2007, a geologist discovered the fossil of an extinct aquatic mammal, called Indohyus, that was about the size of a cat and had hooves and a long tail.*

Scientists think the animal belonged to a group related to cetaceans such as Ambulocetus natans. This creature is considered a "missing link" between artiodactyls — a group of hoofed mammals (even-toed ungulates) that includes hippos, pigs, and cows — and whales, according to the National Science Foundation.

Researchers knew that whales were related to artiodactyls, but until the discovery of this fossil, there were no known artiodactyls that shared physical characteristics with whales. After all, hippos, thought to be cetaceans' closest living relatives, are very different from whales. Indohyus, on the other hand, was an artiodactyl, indicated by the structure of its hooves and ankles, and it also had some similarities to whales, in the structure of its ears, for example.

Genetic evidence also supports the idea that whales evolved from land mammals and provides information about the exact branching of the evolutionary tree. For instance, in 1999, researchers reported in the journal Proceedings of the National Academy of Sciences that according to genetic analysis of "jumping gene" sequences, which copy and paste themselves into genomes, hippos were whales' closest living relatives. Before 1985, researchers thought pigs were more closely related to whales, but this 1999 study overturned that idea, as the Associated Press reported.

*In 2019, researchers reported in the journal Science Advances about which genes within the whale genome were inactivated during the process of the creature's evolution from land mammals, as Science Friday reported. The researchers could tell that certain genes, including one involved in making saliva, had been inactivated because there are remnants of them, which the researchers call genomic fossils, in whale genomes. This indicates that whales evolved from a salivating creature.*

*There's also evidence of cetacean evolution from developmental biology. Developmental biology illustrates the fact that animals that are very different as adults share similarities as embryos because they are evolutionarily related. For example, as embryos, cetaceans started to develop hind limbs, which disappear later in development, while the forelimbs remain and develop into flippers, according to the journal Evolution: Education and Outreach. This suggests that cetaceans evolved from a four-legged ancestor.*

*Is The Theory of Evolution Controversial?*

*Despite the wealth of evidence from the fossil record, genetics and other fields of science, some people still question the theory of evolution's validity. Some politicians and religious leaders denounce the theory, invoking a higher being as a designer to explain the complex world of living things, especially humans.*

*School boards debate whether the theory of evolution should be taught alongside other ideas, such as intelligent design or creationism.*

*Mainstream scientists see no controversy. "A lot of people have deep religious beliefs and also accept evolution," Pobiner said, adding, "there can be real reconciliation."*

*Evolution is well supported by many examples of changes in various species leading to the diversity of life seen today. "Natural selection, or to put it another way — variation, heredity, and differential fitness — is the core theory of modern biology," John Lambshead explains. "It is to biology what, say quantum mechanics and special relativity are to physics or the atomic model is to chemistry."*

What I find interesting is that most of us tend to believe there is only one way or one answer to anything. That is, if evolution is correct, then creationism is debunked, and vice-versa. We must remember that most of us only use 10% of our brain capability. I believe geniuses use 15%. It would stand to reason that we don't really have all the answers.

It should also be noted that it is said that Darwin became a born-again Christian before he died, and insisted "It was just a theory". No matter one's religious beliefs, and no matter what one believes as to how we evolved as a species, all humans are comprised of the basic same cellular makeup. We all have the same basic bodily functions and same basic needs. We are all spiritual beings having a human experience. The Scriptures state how it is unwise to compare yourselves with yourselves, that is to compete with one another, since to those who are given much, much is required of them. (Luke 12:48). This means we all have an accountability and responsibility for this planet, for its resources, and for our gifts, talents, and abilities. We are no better or worse than anyone else. We are to use what we have for the better of ourselves and those around us. This in and of itself makes one great, no matter when and how one was created or evolved.

## Chapter 5. Effects of Competition and Commerce

*Money has never made man happy, nor will it, there is nothing in its nature to produce happiness. The more of it one has the more one wants.*
*- Benjamin Franklin -*

Commerce creates competition through the drive to acquire more and more money. This profit-seeking capitalistic system created thousands of years ago, had a purpose, but is no longer viable, sustainable, and no longer needed. In fact, it is detrimental to the health of the planet and the people.

For example, countries in Africa have been colonized or taken over by other ethnicities and yet in 2021, Africa is still considered their world, but yet it still has poverty, crime, and horrible politics. Give it 60 years and people will believe Asians to be the original indigenous people to Africa, just like they do in Asia now, when it is actually the copper-colored melanin-rich people who are also indigenous to Asia.

This colonization has promulgated for centuries, bringing with it more and more profit-seeking blood suckers. The life blood of the planet has literally and figuratively been withdrawn from the many for the benefit of the few with no substantial deposits to balance the survival accounts. This in and of itself has made the planet unhealthy as a whole.

From an article called "How Healthy Is The World?" By Bjørn Lomborg, published in 2002 in the *British Medical Journal*, Lomborg acknowledges that life expectancy is 76.8 years. Of course, many live much longer such as Cicely Tyson who passed away at 96 and Bette White who at 99 is about to celebrate her 100th birthday. It is expected that by 2080, the life expectancy should reach 80 years. However, as we know, the "elite psychopaths" are disturbed by this and want to reduce the population by at 2/3 of what it is today.

According to Lomborg, this life expectancy is due largely to the improvements in welfare during the last 50 years that include heightened education levels and literacy, more political and civil rights, increased access to technological innovations, and more income that opens up more opportunities to people to allow them to live a better life. However, with all of the increase in life expectancy and better living for most, that is, many are concerned about whether or not there will be enough food for all, how can be conserve energy and utilize it ecologically for the environment, what can be done about the harmful emission of carbon dioxide and its effect on the sun and the planet. Lomberg insists that "these concerns can all be quelled from the simple elimination of our drive toward commerce instead of community". It is a fact that we are continually destroying our forest, trees, soil, and atmosphere for the sake of industry, so we can produce more and more products and engage in more financial transactions to maintain a system that does not work to sustain life on this planet anymore.

(Source: BMJ: British Medical Journal , Dec. 21 - 28, 2002, Vol. 325, No. 7378 (Dec. 21 - 28, 2002), pp. 1461-1464; Published by: BMJ Stable; http://www.jstor.com/stable/25453216)

There was a study done by Muriel Niederle who published her findings in *The American Economic Review* by the American Economic Association in 2017. (Source: https://www.jstor.org/stable/44250372). According to the study, Muriel Niederle explains that "competitiveness is a psychological attribute that predicts math and science choices in school and that gender differences in competitiveness can help account for gender differences in these education choices". She also states that competitiveness predicts economic outcomes. I ask, would women be less likely to explore and study math and sciences if earnings and competition were not a factor?

In her study and experiment, they used a model whereby the subject with the highest performance received $2 for every correct problem while everyone else received no payment. I ask, why is this type of reinforcement constantly used and a made a factor – punishment and reward from external contrived sources. We call it "incentive". Do people really need this type of incentive?

Niederle found that men had significantly higher beliefs about their relative performance than women. Does this imply that men have an innate drive to compete or is this instilled by parents and society from a patriarchal society, mostly governed by and ruled by men? According to Niederle, performance and beliefs and risk aversion play only a minor role. Below are some of the highlights from Niederle's study:

- Specifically, in the Netherlands, 15-year-olds who are in the pre-university level choose between four study tracks for their last three years of school: a Math, Biology, Economics and Literature track. This ordering

of math and science intensity is also the order of prestige, where the best performing children go. Dutch boys are more likely than girls to go to more prestigious tracks, generating a gender gap in math and science education.
- To address the external relevance of competitiveness, more competitive children select more prestigious tracks.
- Knowing their competitiveness is a better predictor of their track choice than knowing their gender.
- To correlate competitiveness with earnings, two years later more "competitive" individuals earn 9 percent more than their less competitive peers, an effect similar to that of gender.
- Given the role of competitiveness on the economic gender gap, one potential policy implication might be to "change the women", make them more competitive and have then "lean in".
- Addressing the role of flexibility in choices, they found that it may lead to institution or market design that may reduce the role of competitiveness and as such reduce the gender gap outcomes.

The conclusion was that women are more ready to

compete against other women than against men. Of course we see this not just in sports. This type of competition carries over in other areas of life, especially when it comes to dating and relationships. Some think of this as normal behavior. However, do we really need to compete for anything? Why must there be winners and losers? Can our advanced creative minds that have engineered amazing technology dare to engineer everyday win-win situations in all aspect of our lives? It would take shaking off stereotypes and eons of brainwashing and conditioning.

In an article called "Unhealthy Competition" by Nick Seddon, published in 2007 by *The Institute for the Study of Civil Society*, Seddon argues, that with respect to the nationalized monopoly of health care providers, competition is the best way to improve a service of whatever kind. He argues that those who object to competition on the basis of the assumption that those who advocate it "are simplistically wedded to the private sector". He states that it "is not the strength of the private sector versus the weakness of the public sector which informs a belief in the importance of markets, so much as a belief that competition improves supply." However, if all health care was free to everyone, those who truly care about treating and helping others would be in this profession. They would not be in it for monetary gain. The system itself would not be toward monetary gain and therefore no need for monopolies and also no need for competition. The simple rule would be "do unto others as you would have them do unto you". (Source: https://www.jstor.org/stable/resrep36364.11).

## One Avenue To A Viable Solution: The Zeitgeist Movement

One of the best solutions to the problems the world experience with the need to compete through this system of capitalism is expressed thoroughly in The Zeitgeist Movement (TZM). The definition of the word "zeitgeist" is to encourage and urge change in the dominant intellectual, moral and cultural climate of the time. The Zeitgeist group seeks to propel us to a higher mindset. They believe, as do I, that our old, useless and now primitive ways and means are not profitable for the planet nor each other.

The following excerpts are taken directly from The Zeitgeist Movement book entitled The Zeitgeist Movement Defined – *Realizing A New Train of Thought*. I believe they succinctly give us a road toward a viable and plausible change:

*Information can only be evaluated correctly through a systematic process of comparison to other physically verifiable evidence as to its proof or lack thereof.*

*There is no statement more erroneous than the declaration that "this is my idea". Such notions are byproducts of a material culture that has been reinforced in seeking physical rewards, usually via money, in exchange for the illusion of their "proprietary" creations. Very often an ego association is culminated as well where an individual claims prestige about their "credit" for an idea or invention. Neither the great political and financial power structures of the world, nor the specialization-blinded professionals, nor the population in general realize that...it is now highly feasible to take care of everybody on earth at a "higher standard of living than any have ever known". It no longer has to be you or me. Selfishness is unnecessary and henceforth [non]rationalizable as mandated by survival. War is obsolete.*

*For instance, the current social model, while perpetuating enormous levels of corrosive economic inefficiency in general, as will be described in further essays, also intrinsically supports one economic group or "class" of people over another, perpetuating technically unnecessary imbalance and high relative deprivation. This could be called "economic bigotry" in its effect and it is no less insidious than discrimination rooted in gender, ethnicity, religion, creed or the like. However, this inherent bigotry is really only a part of a larger condition that could be termed "structural violence", illuminating a broad spectrum of built in suffering, inhumanity and deprivation that is simply accepted as normality today by an uninformed majority. This context of violence stretches much farther and deeper than many. As a broader example, a great deal of social study has now been done on the subject of "social inequality" and its effects on public health. As will be discussed more so in further essays, there is a vast array of physical and mental health problems that appear to be born out of this condition, including propensities towards physical violence, heart disease, depression, educational deficiency and many, many other detriments that have a truly social consequence which can affect us all.*

*This new civil rights movement is about the sharing of human knowledge and our technical ability to not only solve problems, but to facilitate a scientifically derived social system that actually optimizes our potential and well-being. Anything less will create unnecessary imbalance and social destabilization and constitute what could be considered a hidden form of oppression. TZM's broad actions could be summarized as to diagnose, educate and create.*

## Chapter 6. Making The Universal Move To A Better Economy

*Man cannot discover new oceans unless he has the courage to lose sight of the shore.*
*- Andre Gide -*

Most everyone would agree that we have a serious problem, especially with inflation, the rising costs, and an economic system that can no longer sustain itself and no longer meet the needs of the people and the planet. Well, the first step to getting to a cure for anything is to make the correct diagnosis. So, what is the diagnosis? The Zeitgeist Movement is already on top of this:

> *Diagnosis is "the identification of the nature and cause of anything." To properly diagnose the causal condition of the vast social and ecological problems common to modern culture is not merely to complain about them or criticize the actions of people or particular institutions, as is frequent today. A true diagnosis must seek out the lowest causal denominator possible and work at that level for resolution.*
> 
> *The central problem is that there is often what could be called a truncated frame of reference, where shortsighted, misdiagnosis of given consequences persists. For instance, the traditional, established*

> solution to the reformation of human behavior for many so-called "criminal acts" is often punitive incarceration. Yet, this says nothing about the deeper motivation of the "criminal" and why their psychology led to such acts to begin with.
> 
> At that level, such a resolution becomes more complex and reliant upon the synergetic relationship of their physical and cultural culmination over time. This is no different than when a person dies of cancer, as it isn't really the cancer that kills them in the literal sense, as the cancer itself is the product of other forces.

Michael Tellinger, in his book <u>UBUNTU: Contributionism</u>, not only gives the diagnosis of the world's central problem, he also shows how to solve the problem. Tellinger and I both agree that society's ills today begin and end with this profit-seeking blood-sucking capitalistic system. It accounts for 99% of the problems.

> Most people are under the incorrect assumption that money is the consequence of human evolution and thousands of years of barter and trade.
> 
> As hard as this may be for some people to accept, that is an incorrect assumption.
> 
> Meticulous scrutiny of our human history shows very clearly that money was introduced several thousand years ago, by a

small group of royal political elite as the supreme tool of control and enslavement of the masses.

Since the very first introduction of money this small group of very powerful individuals have controlled the printing and supply of money, and thereby control the events on planet Earth.

7 Points We Must Come To Terms With About Money:

- Money is the obstacle to all progress
- Money is the cause of all misery on Earth
- Money is the major contributing factor to the gross separation and segregation in Society
- Money is the cause of 99% of crime
- Money causes families to fall apart
- Money is the driving force behind the SEVEN deadly sins - ego, gluttony, jealousy, greed, envy, lust and all the ugliest aspects of humanity
- Money has been the motive behind most of the wars of the past 2000 years and funded by the bankers, often funding both sides for maximum profit and control.

The solution is very clear.

Create a new system in which money is no longer necessary and very soon we will remove money from society completely and nobody will even realize that we no longer use it - because our lives will be filled with bliss and joy on every level."

There is much more detail in the

UBUNTU book by Michael Tellinger and in his YouTube presentations on the origins of money.

(Source: https://www.amazon.com/UBUNTU-Contributionism-Blueprint-Human-Prosperity-ebook/dp/B00GYXGY52/ref=sr_1_7?crid=2ZFHTABMG0KMS&keywords=UBUNTU&qid=1647968736&s=books&sprefix=ub%2Cstripbooks%2C1349&sr=1-7)

After diagnosing the problem, the next step Zeitgeist movement recommends toward healing our world is to educate. They define the word educate as "an open-ended train of thought, not rigid text of static ideas." The focus is on "train of thought", not institutionalized brain washing, mind control, and rigid systems of rote memory to regurgitate back useless information and statistics. People are naturally creative and critical thinking beings and can solve problems, revise and update systems as needed. This education or erudition must result in a change of mindset where we are all seen as parts of the whole and know that our planet and our survival depends on our knowledge and actions based on this concept.

This leads to the next step the Zeitgeist Movement

recommends, and that is to create. This creation is based on the following realizations:

- *Optimum economic efficiency A natural law/ resource based economy*
- *Old, useless religions and trains of thought:*
- *Such "established institutions", as they could be called, often wish to maintain permanence due to reasons of ego, power, market income or general psychological comfort. This problem is, in many ways, at the core of our social paralysis.*
- *The real revolution is the revolution of values.*

It should be noted that the Zeitgeist Movement makes special emphasis on the "scientific method". While I agree, I also acknowledge that along with the logic and reasoning must come the esoteric, intuitive, and spiritual. "The things that are not seen are more real than the things that are seen."

This planet and the people on it are inter-connected. The "elite psychopaths" understand this perfectly, however, they are only bent on destroying this planet and its people. They see themselves as superior beings (a "better species") and the rest of us as unnecessary and detrimental to their existence. They have already begun to colonize other planets and have made safe, secure communities for them and their military forces underground. While we deal above ground with their imposed chemtrails, 5G, carbon monoxide poisoning, human trafficking, "plandemics", and other horrific atrocities, they have created lovely havens for themselves.

Today, they have coined the phrase "sustainability", but the "elite psychopaths" do not see this the same as we do. The Zeitgeist Movement explains it completely:

> *While the notion of "sustainability" might be typically associated with technical processes, eco-theory and engineering today, we often forget that our values and beliefs precede all such technical applications. Therefore, we need our cultural orientation to be sustainable to begin with and that awareness can only come from a valid recognition of the laws of nature to which we are bound. That noted and in the context of this essay, specifically the points about emergence & symbiosis, it could be generalized that any belief system that (a) does not have built into it the allowance for that entire belief system itself to be altered or even made completely obsolete due to new information, is an unsustainable belief system; and (b) any belief system that supports isolation and*

*division, supporting the integrity of one segment or group over another is also an unsustainable belief system.*

*A powerful yet often overlooked consequence of our environmental vulnerability to adapt to the existing culture is that our very identity and personality is often linked to the institutions, practices, trends and hence values we are born into and exist in. This psychological adaptation and inevitable familiarity creates a comfort zone which, over time, can be painful to disrupt, regardless of how well reasoned the data standing to the contrary of what we believe may be.*

*The most common classification of such arguments are "projections" and it becomes clear very often that such opponents are actually more concerned with defending their psychological identity rather than objectively considering a new perspective Our emotional dispositions make it very difficult for us to accept certain propositions, no matter how strong the evidence in their favor. And since all proof depends upon the acceptance of certain propositions as true, no proposition can be proved to be true to one who is sufficiently determined not to believe it.*

*For example, in the so-called democracies of the world, a "president", or the equivalent, is a common point of focus with respect to the quality of a country's governance. A large amount of attention is* spent toward such a figure, his perspectives and actions. Yet, seldom does one step back and ask:

"Why do we have a president to begin with?"

"How is his/her power as an institutional figure justified as an optimized manner of social governance?"

"Is it not a contradiction of terms to claim a democratic society when the public has virtually no real say with respect to the actions of the president once he or she is elected?"

Such questions are seldom considered as people tend, again, to adapt to their culture without objection, assuming it is "just the way it is". Such static orientations are almost universally a result of cultural tradition and, as Cohen and Nagel point out, it is very difficult to communicate a new, challenging idea to those who are "sufficiently determined not to believe it".

Such traditional presuppositions, held as empirical, are likely a root source of personal and social retardation in the world today. This phenomenon, coupled with an educational system that constantly reinforces such established notions through its institutions of "academia", further seals this cultural inhibition and compounds the hindrance to relevant change.

TZM's advocated train of thought, on the other hand, sources advancements in *human studies. It finds, for example, that social stratification, which is inherent to the capitalist/ market model, to actually be a form of indirect violence against the vast majority as a result of the evolutionary psychology we humans naturally possess. It generates an unnecessary form of human suffering on many levels, which is destabilizing and, by implication, technically unsustainable.*

*TZM's advocated logic, on the other hand, relates the fact that the practice of universal, individual ownership of goods is environmentally inefficient, wasteful and ultimately unsustainable as a practice. This supports a restrictive system behavior and a great deal of unnecessary deprivation, and hence crime is common in societies with an unequal distribution of resources.*

*For example, when discussing the organization of a new social system, people often project their current values and concerns into the new model without considering the vast change of context inherent which would likely nullify such concerns immediately. A common straw-man projection in this context would be that in a society where material production [was] based upon technological application directly and not an exchange system requiring paid human labor, people would have no incentive to do anything and therefore the model would fail as nothing would get done. This kind of argument is without testable validity with respect to the human sciences and is really an intuitive assumption originating from the current cultural climate where the economic system coerces all humans into labor roles for survival (income/profit). This often occurs regardless of one's personal interest or social utility, often generating a psychological distortion with respect to motivation.*

*In the words of Margaret Mead: "If you look closely you will see that almost anything that really matters to us, anything that embodies our deepest commitment to the way human life should be lived and cared for, depends on some form of volunteerism."*

*In a 1992 Gallup Poll, more than 50% of American adults (94 million Americans) volunteered time for social causes, at an average of 4.2 hours a week, for a total of 20.5 billion hours a year. It has also been found in studies that repetitive, mundane jobs lend themselves more to traditional rewards such as money, whereas money doesn't seem to motivate innovation and creativity. In later essays, the idea of mechanization/ automation applied to mundane labor to free the human being will be discussed, expressing how the labor-for-income system is outdated and restrictive of not only industrial potential and efficiency, but also human potential and creativity overall.*

*Similarly, and final example here of the "straw-man", is the confusion about how a transition to a new system could happen at all. In fact, many tend to dismiss TZM's proposals on that basis alone, simply because they don't understand how it can happen. This argument, in principle, is the same reasoning as the example of a sick man who is seeking treatment for his illness but does not know where he can get such treatment, when it would be available, or what the treatment is. Does his lack of knowing how and when stop his need to seek? No - not if he wants to be healthy.*

*Given the dire state of affairs on this planet, humanity must also keep seeking and a path will inevitably come clear. The xenophobic and mafia-like mentality indigenous to the nation-state today, often in the form of "patriotism", is a source of severe destabilization and inhumanity in general, not to mention, again, a substantial loss of technical efficiency.*

*Understanding that Earth is a symbiotic/synergistic "system" with resources existing in all areas, coupled with the provably inherent, underlying causal scientific order that exists, in many ways, as a logical "guide" for the human species to align with for the greatest societal efficacy, we find that our larger context as a global society transcends all notions of traditional/cultural division, including having no loyalty to a country, corporation*

> *or even "political" tradition.*
>
> *If an "economy" is about increasing efficiency in meeting the needs of the human population while working to further sustainability and prosperity, then our economic operations must take this into account and align with the largest relevant "system" that we can understand. So again, from this perspective, the nation-state entities are clearly false, arbitrary divisions perpetuated by cultural tradition, not logical, technical efficiency."*

Finally, the Zeitgeist Movement insists that we must have a change in our values if we are to survive. Our present-day values center mostly around continual and optimal competition with each other and those whom we see as "enemies":

> *The broad organization of society today is based on multi-level human competition. Nation-states compete against each other for economic/physical resources; corporate market entities compete for profit/market-share; and average workers compete for wage providing occupations/income and hence personal survival itself. Within this competitive ethic is a basic psychological propensity to disregard the wellbeing of others and the habitat. The very nature of competition is about having advantage over*

*others for personal gain and hence, needless to say, division and exploitation are common attributes of the current social order.*

*Interestingly, virtually all so-called "corruption" which we may define as "crime" in the world today is based upon the very same mentality assumed to guide "progress" in the world through the competitive interest. It is no wonder, in fact, given this framework, that various other detrimental, superficial social divisions are still pervasive such as race, religion, creed, class or xenophobic bias. This divisive baggage from early, fear-oriented stages of our cultural evolution simply has no working basis in the physical reality and serves now only to hinder progress, safety and sustainability.*

*The historical pattern of conflict cannot be considered in mere isolation. Detailed reference to the conditions and circumstances are needed. In fact, it's likely accurate to say that the dominance/conflict propensity which is clearly a possible reaction for nearly all humans in our need for self-preservation and survival in general is being provoked by pressures rather than being the source of any negative reaction.*

*When we wonder how the massive Nazi army were able to morally justify their actions in World War II, we often forget the enormous propaganda campaign put out by that regime which worked to exploit this*

*essentially biological vulnerability.*
*The bottom line is that things have changed in the world today and your self-interest is now only as good as your societal interest. Being competitive and going out for yourself, "beating" others only has a negative consequence in the long-term, for it is denying awareness of the synergistic system we are bound within. A cheaply made nuclear power plant in Japan might not mean much to people in America. However, if that plant was to have a large scale technical failure, the fallout and pollution might make its way over to American homes, proving that you are never safe in the long run unless you have a global consciousness.*

## Warfare – The Most Destructive & Devastating Form of Competition

The Zeitgeist movement has a lot to contribute on the subject of warfare:

*The days of practical warfare are long over. New technology on the horizon has the ability to create weapons that will make the atom bomb look like a roman catapult in destructive power. Centuries ago, warfare could at least be minimized to the warring parties overall. Today, the entire world is threatened. There are over 23,000 Nuclear Weapons today, which could wipe out the human population many times over.*
*In many ways, our very social*

*maturity is being questioned at this time. Battles with only sticks and stones as weapons could tolerate a great deal of human distortion and malicious intent. However, in a world of nano-tech weapons that could be constructed in a small lab with enormous destructive power, our expanded self-interest needs to take hold and the institution of war needs to be systematically shutdown. In order to do this, nations must technically unify and share their resources and ideas, not hoard them for competitive self-betterment, which is the norm today.*

*Institutions like the United Nations have become complete failures in this regard because they naturally become tools of empire building due to the underlying nature of country divisions and the socioeconomic dominance of the property/ monetary/ competition based system orientation. It is not enough to simply gather global "leaders" at a table to discuss their problems. The structure itself needs to change to support a different type of interaction between these regional "groups" where the perpetual "threat" inherent between nation-states is removed.*

*In the end, there is no empirical ownership of resources or ideas. Just as all ideas are serially developed across culture through the group mind, the resources of the planet are equally as transient in their function and scientifically defined as to their possible purposes. The Earth is a single* system, along with the laws of nature that govern it. Either human society recognizes and begins to act and organize on this inherent logic, or we suffer in the long run. The overall basis of the market concept has to do fundamentally with assumptions related to human behavior, traditional values and an intuitive view of history - not emergent reasoning, actual public health measures, technical capacity or ecological responsibility. It is a non-technical, philosophical approach, which merely assumes that human decisions made through its internal logic (and incentive system), will produce a responsible, sustainable and humane outcome, driven by the illusive notion of "freedom of choice" which, on the scale of societal functionality, appears tantamount to organizational anarchy. the "price mechanism", which is the central catalyst for economic unfolding today, is inherently anarchistic due to the lack of efficient system relationships within macro-industrial practices. Production, distribution and resource allocation is not "strategic" in a technical, physical sense by any stretch of the imagination – the only strategy employed, which is the defining context of "efficiency" in the market economy, has to do with the profit and loss/labor cost/expense type monetary parameters which have no relationship to physical efficiency at all.

## Can We Truly Evolve?

Man can and must evolve for his own survival. The Zeitgeist Movement explains:

> *Moreover, while it is clear we humans still appear to maintain "hardwired", predictable reactions for raw, personal survival, we have also proven the ability to evolve our behaviors through thought, awareness and education, allowing us to, in fact, control/overcome those impulsive, primitive reactions, if the conditions for such are supported and reinforced. This is an extremely important distinction and is what separates the variance of human beings from their lesser evolved primate family in many ways.*
>
> *In the end, the most relevant issue is stress. Our genes, biology and evolutionary psychology might have some hang-ups, but they are nothing compared to the environmental disorder we have created in our culture. The enormity of now unnecessary stress in the world today – debt, job insecurity, increasing health risks both mental and physiological - and many other issues have created a climate of unease that has been increasingly making people sick and upset. If we were faced with an option to adapt our society in a way that could "provably" better public health, increase social stability, generate abundance and help sustainability, would we not just do it?*

*To think human beings are simply incompatible with methods that can increase their standard of living and health is extremely unlikely. but the poverty condition that enables it to flourish. However, the causality doesn't stop there. We then need to ask the question: "what is causing the poverty?"*

*A more abstract "micro" example would be human development problems when adverse pressures in family or community structures occur. Imagine a single mother who, due to the financial need to raise her child, must work for income a great deal in order to make ends meet, limiting her availability for the child personally. The pressures not only reduce needed support and guidance for the child's development, she also develops tendencies for depression and anxiety due to the ongoing stress of debt, bills and the like, and frustration-driven abuse begins to materialize in the family. This then causes severe emotional loss in the child and the development of neurotic and unhealthy mental states emerge, such as a propensity for drug addiction. Years later, still suffering from the pain felt in those early periods, the now adult child dies in a heroin overdose. Question: what caused the overdose? The heroin? The mother's influence? Or the economic circumstance the mother found herself which disallowed balance and thoughtful care of her child?*

*For example, child abuse, both physical and emotional, along with increasingly difficult levels of personal stress, have a direct correlation to both premeditated and impulsive acts of violence and while men have a statistically higher propensity towards violence due to largely endocrinological characteristics that, while not causing violent reactions, can exaggerate them upon the stress influence, the common theme is the influence of the environment and culture. This is not to discount the relationship of hormones or even possibly genetic propensities, but to show that at the origin of this behavior is clearly not our biology, but the condition upon which a human exists and the experiences endured.*

*Other common assumptions of causality, such as "instinct" are also far too abstract and vague to hold any operational validity. Dr. Gilligan states: "I am suggesting that the only way to explain the causes of violence, so that we can learn how to prevent it, is to approach violence as a problem in public health and preventive medicine, and to think of violence as a symptom of life-threatening pathology, which, like all form of illness, has an etiology or cause, a pathogen."*

*In Dr. Gilligan's diagnosis he makes it very clear that the greatest cause of violent behavior is social inequality, highlighting the influence of shame and humiliation as an emotional characteristic of those who engage in violence. Thomas Scheff, [an] emeritus professor of sociology in California stated that "shame was the social emotion". Shame and humiliation can be equated with the feelings of stupidity, inadequacy, embarrassment, foolishness, feeling exposed, insecurity and the like – all largely social or comparative in their origin.*

*Needless to say, in a global society with not only growing income disparity but inevitably "self-worth" disparity - since status is touted as directly related to our "success" in our jobs, bank account levels and the like - it is no mystery that feelings of inferiority, shame and humiliation are staples of the culture today.*

*The consequence of those feelings have very serious implications for public health, as noted before, including the epidemic of the behavioral violence we now see today in its various complex forms. Terrorism, local school and church shootings, along with other extreme acts that simply did not exist before in the abstractions they find context today, reveals a unique evolution of violence itself. Dr. Gilligan concludes: "If we wish to prevent violence, then, our agenda is political and economic reform."*

*Human progress, health and success are clearly not defined by the constant influx of market goods, gadgets and material creations for purchase. Public health and wellbeing are based on how we relate to each other and the environment as a whole and market induced stratification is extremely caustic to society. The result is a hidden form of violence against the population and hence the public health issues we see are really civil & human rights issues, since they simply do not need to exist.*

*When we see clear genocide in the world we object strongly on purely moral grounds. But what if there existed a constant genocide that is unseen but very real, perpetuated not by a specific person or group but by disorder born out of stress/effects generated by the traditional method of human interaction and economic ordering that has been created and codified?*

*Slavery, classism, xenophobia, racism, sexism, subjugation and many other divisive & exploitative notions still common to human cultural history will be found to have kernels of origin or perpetuation in many generally accepted economic philosophies to one degree or another. History is fairly clear with respect to how the social condition is groomed by the prevailing economic assumptions of a given period and this broad sociological consideration is sadly not given much gravity in the world today when thinking about why the world is the way it is and why we think the way we do.*

*As a preliminary point, a point which*

*will reemerge later in this essay, there has commonly been a duality noted in most modern economic thought where the "capitalist free market", meaning the "free" actions of independent producers, laborer and traders, working in aggregate to buy, sell and employ, is to be contrasted to that of the "state", meaning a unified system of delegated power that has the capacity to set legal policy and economic mandates that can inhibit the actions of the "free market" through interference.*

*Most economic debates today revolved around this duality on one level or another with the "laissez-faire" interests, or those who wish to have a completely non-regulated market economy, constantly at war with the "statists", or those who think some kind of centralized government control and decision making over economic planning and policy is best.*

*Today, the dominant and largely accepted microeconomic perspective is that all human behavior is reducible to rational, strategic attempts to maximize either profits or gain and to avoid pain or loss. Ever expansive utilitarian arguments of this nature continue to be used to morally justify competitive, market capitalism.*

*One example of this is the notion of "voluntarism" and the suggestion that all acts in the market are never coerced and therefore everyone is free to make their own decisions for their own gain or loss. This*

> *idea is extremely common today, as though such "free exchanges" existed in a void with no other synergistic pressures; as though the pressures of survival in a system with clear tendencies toward basic class warfare and strategic scarcity would not generate an inherent coercion to force laborers to submit to capitalist exploitation.*

**Do We Really Own Anything?**

Each of us is born into this world and onto this particular planet. We are naked when we enter, bringing absolutely nothing with us except our inherited DNA, memories of past lives (for those who believe), and our soon-to-be-developed skills, abilities, gifts, and talents – all which we owe to our ascendants. Everything, every resource, every equipment, every supply, every technology is already here. We can use our talents, gifts, and skills to add, revise, improve, and procreate. There is nothing new under the sun. What has been will soon be again. We are born into a cycle of life where we utilize our time and space to discover, learn, create, educate, and enjoy. All the other headaches and heartaches man brings upon himself because of his lust, greed, ego, and vanity, not realizing this place is his/her training ground to rid himself/herself of these types of imperfections to prepare him/her for the next experience.

Instead, most of us are conditioned to think we need to "own" things, and even people, which we can surely not take with us when we depart. The Zeitgeist Movement explains:

> *This natural-rights theory of property makes the creative effort of an isolated, self-sufficing individual the basis of ownership vested in him. In so doing it overlooks the fact that there is no isolated, self-sufficing individual. Production takes place only in society - only through the co-operation of an industrial community. This industrial community may be large or small...but it always comprises a group large enough to contain and transmit the traditions, tools, technical knowledge, and usages without which there can be no industrial organization and no economic relation of individuals to one another or to their environment...There can be no production without technical knowledge; hence no accumulation and no wealth to be owned, in severalty or otherwise. And there is no technical knowledge apart from an industrial community. Since there is no individual production and no individual productivity, the natural-rights preconception...reduces itself to absurdity, even under the logic of its own assumptions.*

**Identity, Normality, and Disorder**

The connotative definition of the terms Identity, Normality, and Disorder come from our social structuring and conditioning, mostly what we impose upon ourselves, not necessarily from our genes. The Zeitgeist Movement explains:

> *Likewise, just as genes can mutate in ways that are detrimental to their host, such as the phenomenon of cancer, so can memes with respect to ideological/sociological transmissions, generating mental frameworks that serve as detriments to the host (or society). It is here where the term "disorder" is introduced. A disorder is defined as "a derangement or abnormality of function". Therefore, when it comes to social operation, a disorder would imply institutionalized ideological frameworks that are out of alignment with the larger governing system. In other words, they are inaccurate with respect to the context in which they attempt to exist, often creating imbalance and detrimental destabilization.*
>
> *Of course, history is full of initially destabilizing, transitioning ideas and this ongoing intellectual evolution is clearly natural and necessary to the human condition as there is no such thing as an "absolute" understanding. However, the differentiation to be made here is the fact that when ideas persist for a long enough period, they often create emotional*

> connections on the personal ("identity") level and institutional establishments on the cultural level, which tend to perpetuate a kind of circular reinforcement, generally resisting change and adaptation.

## Self-Preservation Paralysis

According to the Zeitgeist Movement, our world suffers from a "self-preservation paralysis" inflicted upon us:

> While each of us generally wishes to survive and do so in a healthy state, naturally prepared to defend that survival when need be, self-preservation in the current socioeconomic condition unnecessarily extends this tendency in ways that severely inhibit social progress and problem resolution. In fact, it could be said that this short-term preservation occurs often at the cost of long-term integrity.
>
> The most obvious example of this has to do with the fundamental nature of seeking and maintaining income, the lifeblood of the market system and, by extension, human survival. Once a business succeeds in gaining market share, typically supporting employees along with the owners, the business naturally gravitates to an interest to preserve that income generating market share at all costs. Deep value associations are generated since the business is not just an arbitrary entity that produces a good or

*service - it is now a means of life support for everyone involved.*

*The result is a constant, socially debilitating battle, not only with the competitors who also seek the same consumer market, but with innovation and change itself. While technological progress is a constant, fluid progression on the scientific level, the market economy sees this emergence as a threat in the context of existing, currently profitable ideas. Vast levels of historical "corruption", cartel and monopoly generation and other defensive moves of existing businesses can be found throughout history, each act working to secure income production regardless of the social costs.*

*Another example has to do with the psychological neurosis built out of the credit-based reward incentive inherent to the market system. While it is intellectually clear that no single person invents anything given the reality that all knowledge is serially generated and invariably cumulative over time, the market economy's characteristic of "ownership" creates a tendency not only to reduce information flow via patents and "trade secrets", it also reinforces the idea of "intellectual property", despite the true fallacy of the notion itself.*

*On the value system level, this has mutated into the notion of "credit" entitlement and hence often "ego" associations to presented ideas or "inventions". In the world today, this phenomenon has taken a life of its own with a tendency for many who contribute often seeking status elevating "credit" for the idea, even though they are, again, clearly part of a continuum larger than themselves. While appreciation for the time and labor of a given person working towards the progress of an idea is a productive social incentive and fundamental to our sense of purpose in action, the perversion of intellectual ownership and all its contrived attributes extend this operant satisfaction into distortion.*

*In fact, on the largest scale of knowledge culmination, such acts of "appreciation" inevitably become irrelevant in the memory of history. Today, for instance, when we use a modern computer to assist our lives, we seldom think about the thousands of years of intellectual study that discovered the core scientific dynamics related, nor the enormous amount of cumulative time spent by virtually countless people to facilitate the "invention" of such a tool, in its current form. It is only in the context of manifest ego and monetary reward security that this becomes a "natural" value issue with respect to the market system. If people do not claim "credit", they will not be rewarded and hence they will not gain survival from that contribution in the market. So, the condition has compounded this neurosis that is invariably stifling towards progress via the sharing of knowledge.*

*Furthermore, disorders associated with market "self-preservation" can take many other forms, including the use of government as a tool, the pollution of academia and information itself (since educational institutions are supported by income as well), and even common interpersonal relationships. The fear inherent to the loss of livelihood naturally overrides almost everything and even the most "ethical" or "moral" person, when faced with the risk of non-survival, can usually justify actions that would be traditionally called "corrupt". This pressure is constant and is the source, in part, of the vast co-called "criminality" and social paralysis we see today.*

## Competition, Exploitation and Class Warfare

The self-preservation paralysis stretches its devastating tentacles, claws its way, and transforms itself into competition, exploitation and class warfare. The Zeitgeist Movement explains:

*Building on the prior point, exploitation, which is inherent to the competitive frame of mind, has permeated the very core of what it means to "succeed" in general. We see this "taking advantage" rhetoric in many facets of our lives. The act of manipulation and exploitation for competitive gain has become an underlying force in modern culture, extending far beyond the context of the market system.*

*The attitude of seeing others and the world as merely a means for oneself or a particular group to "conquer" and keep ahead of is now a driving psychological distortion to be found in romantic relationships, friendships, family structures, nationalism and even how we relate to the habitat we exist within - where we seek to exploit and disregard the physical environment's resources for short term personal gain and advantage. All elements of our lives are necessarily viewed from the perspective of "what can I get out of it personally?"*

*A study performed at the Department of Psychology at the University of California, Berkeley, in 2011 found that: "...upper-class individuals behave more unethically than lower-class individuals...upper-class individuals were more likely to break the law while driving, relative to lower-class individuals. In follow-up laboratory studies, upper-class individuals were more likely to exhibit unethical decision-making tendencies, take valued goods from others, lie in a negotiation, cheat to increase their chances of winning a prize, and endorse unethical behavior at work than were lower-class individuals. Mediator and moderator data demonstrated that upper class individuals' unethical tendencies are accounted for, in part, by their more favorable attitudes toward greed."*

*Studies of this nature are very interesting as they reveal that the common human nature argument in its extreme context, that of people inevitably "being competitive and exploitative", when defending the current social system, is bypassed. Class relationships are not genetic relationships, even though the nuances of individual propensities could be argued. This study expresses a cultural phenomenon overall since it is axiomatic to assume that the general attitude of disregard for external negative consequences, or so-called "unethical behavior" expressed by the upper class, is a result of the type of values needed to achieve the position of actually making it to the "upper class".*

*In common poetic rhetoric, this intuition has held true for centuries, with the observation that those who achieve "success" in the business sense, are often "desensitized" and "ruthless". There appears to be a general loss of empathy by those who achieve such "success" and it is intuitively obvious why this is the case, given the value system disorder of competitive disregard inherent to the market system psychology. Overall, the more caring and empathic you are, the less likely you are to succeed financially - no different from a general sport where you are not going to help an opposing player achieve their goals for it means you are more likely to lose.*

*Overall, the lower classes are found to be more socially humane in many ways. For example, it has also been found that the poor give a higher percentage of their income (4.3%) to charity than rich people (2.1%). A 2010 study found that: "...lower class individuals proved to be more generous... charitable... trusting...and helpful...compared with their upper class counterparts. Mediator and moderator data showed that lower class individuals acted in a more prosocial fashion because of a greater commitment to egalitarian values and feelings of compassion. Implications for social class, prosocial behavior, and economic inequality are discussed."*

*A study conducted by the Chronicle of Philanthropy using tax deduction data from the Internal Revenue Service, showed that households earning between $50,000 and $75,000 a year give an average of 7.6% of their discretionary income to charity. That compares to 4.2% for people who make $100,000 or more. In some of the wealthiest neighborhoods, with a large share of people making $200,000 or more a year, the average giving rate was 2.8%.*

**Success & Status**

How do we define success? Although it would seem this would be subjective to each individual, this profit-seeking capitalistic system lends itself to stroke the ego and vanity through giving people a sense of monetary success and elite status, further fueling the "self-preservation paralysis". The Zeitgeist Movement explains:

> *Underlying the capitalist model is an implied assumption that those who contribute the most must gain the most. In other words, it is assumed that to become say, a billionaire, you must have done something important and helpful for society. Of course, this is clearly untrue. The vast majority of extremely wealthy people originate their wealth out of mechanisms that are not socially contributive on any direct, creative level when broken down and analyzed. The act of engineering, problem solving and creative innovation almost always occurs on the level of the laborer in the lower echelons of the corporate complex, only to be capitalized upon by those at the top (owners) who are skilled at the contrived game of generating a "market". This is not to discount the intelligence or hard work of those who hold vast wealth, but to show that the rewards of the system are displaced, allocated to those who exploit the mechanisms of the market,*

*not those who actually engineer and create. In fact, one of the most rewarded sectors of the global economy today is that of investment and finance.*

*This is a classic example as to be a "hedge fund" manager, moving money around for the mere sake of gaining more money, with zero contribution to creative development, is one of the highest paid occupations in the world today. Likewise, the very notion of "success" in the culture today is measured by material wealth, in and of itself. Fame, power and other gestures of attention go hand in hand with material wealth. To be poor is to be abhorred, while to be rich is to be admired. Across almost the entire social spectrum, those of high levels of wealth are treated with immense respect. Part of this has to do with a system-oriented survival mechanism, such as the personal interest in gaining insight into how to also become such a "success" - but overall it has morphed into a strange fetish where the idea of being rich, powerful and famous, by whatever means necessary, is a guiding force.*

*The value system disorder of rewarding, in effect, generally the most ruthless and selfish in our society, both by financial means and then by public adoration and respect, is one of the most pervasive and insidious consequences of the incentive system inherent to the Capitalist model. It not only works to bypass true interests in types of innovation and problem-solving which inherently do not have monetary return, it also reinforces the market system's own existence, justifying itself by way of high status attainment for those who "win" in the system, regardless of true contribution or the social and environmental costs.*

*Sociologist Thorstein Veblen wrote extensively on this issue, referring to this value "virtue" as predatory: "As the predatory culture reaches a fuller development, there comes a distinction between employments... The "honorable" man must not only show capacity for predatory exploit, but he must also avoid entanglement with occupations that do not involve exploit. The tame employments, those that involve no obvious destruction of life and no spectacular coercion of refractory antagonists, fall into disrepute and are relegated to those members of the community who are defective in the predatory capacity; that is to say, those who are lacking massiveness, agility, or ferocity...Therefore the able-bodied barbarian of the predatory culture, who is mindful of his good name...puts in his time in the manly arts of war and devotes his talents to devising ways and means of disturbing the peace. That way lies honor."*

*William Thompson, in his "An Inquiry into the Principles of the Distribution of Wealth Most Conducive to*

*Human Happiness", restates the reality of this associative influence: "Our next position is, that excessive wealth excites the admiration and the imitation, and in this way diffuses the practice of the vices of the rich, amongst the rest of the community; or produces in them other vices arising out of their relative situation to the excessively rich. On this point, nothing is more obvious than the universal operation of the most common principle of our nature – that of association. The wealth, as a means of happiness...is admired or envied by all; the manner and character connected with the abundance of these good things, always strike the mind in conjunction with them..."*

*Classes and class warfare are a natural outgrowth of this as the value associations to wealth and power, manifest by the current system, become an issue of emotional identity over time. The status interest begins to take on a life of its own and it generates actions of self-preservation on the part of the upper class that seek to maintain (or elevate) their status in ways that might not even relate to money or material wealth anymore. Self-preservation, in this case, extends to a kind of drug addiction. Just as a chronic gambler needs the endorphin rush of winning to feel good, those in the upper class often develop similar compulsions in relationship to the state of their perceived status and wealth.*

*The term "greed" is often used to*

*differentiate between those who exploit modestly and those who exploit excessively. Greed is hence a relative notion, just as being "rich" is a relative notion. The term "relative deprivation" refers to the discontent people feel when they compare their positions to others and realize that they have less of what they believe themselves to be entitled to. This psychological phenomenon knows no end and within the context of the material success incentive system of capitalism, its presence as a severe value system disorder is apparent on the level of mental health. While maintaining a needs meeting, quality standard of living is important for physical and mental health, anything beyond that balance in the context of social comparison has the capacity to create severe neurosis and social distortion. Not only is there no "winning" in the end when it comes to the subjective perception of status and wealth, it often serves to decouple those figures from the majority of the human experience, generating alienation and dehumanization in many ways. This empathic loss has no positive outcome on the social level. The predatory reward values inherent to the market system virtually guarantee endless conflict and abuse.*

  *Of course, the myth is that this neurosis of seeking "more and more" status and wealth is the core driver of social progress and innovation. While there might be some basic truth to this intuitive assumption, the intent, again, is not social contribution but advantage and financial gain. It is like saying being chased by a pack of hungry wolves ready to eat you is good for your health since it is keeping you running. While certain accomplishments are clearly occurring, the guiding force (intent) again has little to do with those accomplishments and the detrimental byproducts and larger-order paralysis inherent nullifies in comparison the idea that the values of competition, material greed and vain status is a legitimate source of societal progress. In fact, epidemiologist Richard Wilkinson has extrapolated a comparison of wealthy nations oriented by the income disparity present in each population. It was found that those nations with the least income disparity actually were more innovative and when we consider that the competitive value drive has a large role with respect to how severe the gap between the rich and poor is, it is axiomatic to consider that the values of egalitarianism and collaboration have more creative power than the traditional economic incentive rhetoric would claim.*

*As a final point in this subsection, the subject of materialism and status can be extended to the similar issue of vanity as well. While a mild deviation from our point, the vanity-based culture we have today finds a direct relationship to these drives for status and measures of "success" rooted in the psychological value incentives inherent to the capitalist system. Given that the value system of "acquisition" is, in fact, necessary for the consumption model to work, it is only natural that marketing and advertising generate dissatisfaction continually, including in the way we feel about our physical appearance. In fact, a study was conducted some years ago on the island of Fiji, in which Western television was introduced to a culture that had never experienced the medium before. By the end of the observation period, the effect of materialistic values and vanity took a powerful toll. A relevant percentage of young women, for example, who prior had embraced the style of healthy weight and full features, became obsessed with being thin. Eating disorders, which were virtually unheard of in this culture, began to spread and women specifically were transformed.*

So, how do we get out of this endless cycle and propel ourselves into a better system for our survival? The next chapter delineates this. We will see that the answer has been there the whole time.

## Chapter 7. The Human Body: A More Effective Economic System

*Our problems are man-made, therefore they may be solved by man. And man can be as big as he wants. No problem of human destiny is beyond human beings.*
*- John F. Kennedy -*

The human body has to be one of the most magnificent and wondrous creations. Within it is the entire universe and galaxy, and exists even within each cell, which is a microcosm of the whole. As the saying goes, "as above, so below; as within, so without." A thorough study of this unique system, the human body, has and will continue to give answers to every question known to man. Every creation is based on some aspect of the human body. For example: cameras from the eyes; drums and other musical instruments from the ears, heartbeat, and vocal chords; computers from the brain; cars and other transportation from the legs and arms.

More importantly, the human body is comprised of the best economic (not monetary) system that has or ever will exist. We need to know ourselves and then learn from ourselves. Everything is based on a give and take relationship, so every organ and every cell is nourished and never goes without. It is only when foreign and unwanted substances disrupt the life of the cells, that a problem exists and the body is put in dis-ease.

There is an unwritten agreement and contract that my mind has with my physical body and all of its functions. I am always a caretaker. I am responsible for daily maintenance and survival. In addition, I am involved in an unwritten networking agreement and contract with all the other living, breathing and thinking organisms on this planet, who also are responsible for their daily maintenance and survival. Contrary to popular belief, we are not in competition with each other, whether for resources or attention. There is more than enough space and resources for all on this planet.

Within the human body, all organs are contained in the 3 types of skin layers: Mesoderm, Ectoderm, and Endoderm. The Mesoderm contains 9 organs and is the middle layer of an embryo in early development, between the endoderm and ectoderm. It can be likened to the Matriarch, the mother, who is always nurturing and interceding to make sure all is well. The Ectoderm contains 6 organs and is the outermost layer of cells or tissue of an embryo in early development, or the parts derived from this, which include the epidermis and nerve tissue. It can be likened to the Patriarch who are the first line of protection and defense for the Matriarch. The Endoderm contains 4 organs and is the layer that gives rise to tissues that form internal structures and organs. It can be likened to the Patriarch who are the second line of protection and defense for the Matriarch.

The great human economic system contains the Digestive and Respiratory System, the Nervous System, and the Circulatory and Excretory System. All of these organs work together from within their own system. They are all very well organized, symbiotic, loyal, responsive, and they continually communicate, associate, and network with each other.

So, already we can see how this system is set up to eliminate competition among its cells. Its "female" and "male" counterparts are distributed to provide all that is needed for all. But, this great economic system gets even better.

There are 7 openings in the body, for nutrient and information intake, and mostly for discharges and gases, and waste. They all communicate with each other. They share resources and information. They work together in a symbiotic relationship. All of the cells belong to one of the organs. However, individual and complete in and of itself, each cells knows it is part of a whole and is dependent on all of the other cells.

Each cell is like a hologram of the entire body. That is, each contains all the data in itself, is independent but works in an interdependent relationship. Each has a specific function but can also assume the role/function of another in emergencies.

Blood is the currency that runs throughout the system. It is pumped through and extends throughout the entire system, leaving no cell unnourished.

Oxygen acts as the exchange mechanism for all transactions. Notice this is give and take. The lungs give out $CO_2$ (carbon dioxide) and take in $O_2$ (oxygen). The human body works synergistically with the environment around it.

Melanin is the substance that creates more currency. Life is in the currency (the blood). This is why melanated people are coveted and needed. However, they are used and abused instead of appreciated by the cancer ("elite psychopaths") that has infiltrated the body. Where melanin does not exist, there is no life. It should be noted here that at the time of the writing of this book, the *Roe v. Wade* [410 U.S. 113 (1973)] decision has been rescinded by The Supreme Court. It is now, once again, illegal for women to have an abortion. It is a known fact that women of color have more abortions than others. According to a study in 2019 by The Center for Disease Control:

> *Among the 30 areas that reported race by ethnicity data for 2019, non-Hispanic White women and non-Hispanic Black women accounted for the largest percentages of all abortions (33.4% and 38.4%, respectively), and Hispanic women and non-Hispanic women in the other race category accounted for smaller percentages (21.0% and 7.2%, respectively)*

The "elite psychopaths" care nothing for human life. It is the pure melanin blood of the babies they are after. At the time of the writing of this book, human trafficking and blood sacrifices of our children is one of the most rampant atrocities that continue. Much talk is heard but no true actions to squash these activities exist. But I digress...

Water cleanses and purifies so the system can run smoothly. This is another part of the environment upon which the body depends for its survival, especially since the body is comprised of 75-80% water.

The body has evolved that in order to maintain its existence, it requires nutrients from food and water sources. The system must be maintained daily within and without. To require people to have to pay for food and water is one of the most atrocious manifestations that has ever existed.

We are those cells with a larger body/organ – each which is a part of the universe. It really is just a cell inside a larger body. Sometimes our minds can't or won't understand this concept. It can be quite overwhelming. However, it tends to put all into the proper perspective, especially when we tend to think that we are all that there is and that the sun rises and sets on our behinds.

It should be noted that the idea of the monetary system came from man's primitive idea of how the human body works. This idea was created thousands of years ago, long before the current scientific research and innovations in technology, and long before enhanced and improved knowledge and awareness of the needs of the people. This monetary system is archaic and no longer works, especially due to a handful of people who either forgot or no longer cared about the needs of others. They are the cancer that exists within the body. Cancerous cells are out of balance and destroy other cells, either not realizing or not caring that it is killing the entire body. Such is the same as those who are killing the entire planet and its people.

## Chapter 8. Our Resource-Based Solution: "MEET & GREET"

> *We cannot solve our problems with the same thinking we used when we created them.*
> *- Albert Einstein -*

The Universal Ma'at has devised a new method that we call "MEET & GREET", something with which everyone who participates in social events should be familiar. MEET stands for Ma'at Energy Exchange & Transfer. This usually occurs within one's local community, family, tribe, or organization, that is, those with whom you have a close association and familiarity. GREET stands for Grand Rising Energy Exchange & Transfer. This occurs of course with those outside of your local parameters and extends worldwide, that is, to those in other communities, families, tribes, and organizations.

This economy takes trust, communication, networking, and interdependency, just like the human body. It is based on energy exchange, not monetary exchange. People are appreciated for and utilize their talents, gifts, and abilities, which are the currency/resources. It is based on the following principles:

- Everyone has something to offer; everyone has something to give.
- No one goes hungry
- No one is homeless
- No one works/slaves for the basic necessities of life
- People are not consumed with making paperless or virtual money or owing and possessing anything
- All is free and accessible, BUT must be maintained
- People are caretakers not owners
- People help each other and share
- People do not hoard or take from anyone
- People are geared toward discovering, creating, building, and learning about themselves and the world/universe around them
- People share their knowledge and information – they exchange resources
- People do not fear the unknown
- People appreciate differences because it increases availability of energy exchange
- There is no need for patents
- There is no need for big government

- People work and live to benefit their families, their communities, their environment, and the planet
- People are free to love unconditionally
- People protect each other from those who are evil (those who do not want to live and let live)
- People have no need to harm each other
- People have conquered their fears
- People have no need to possess or try to possess another person

## Chapter 9. Eliminating Our Worst Enemy: FEAR

*Challenges make you discover things about yourself that you never really knew.*
*- Cicely Tyson -*

One of the underlying reasons for most of us who resist change, even for the better, is fear. We fear the unknown instead of embracing it. Our responses seem to be: fright, fight, and flight. This has been proven on a number of occasions and it is further drilled into our heads in the media, especially TV sitcoms and movies. However, I propose another response that has also been proven, and with practice, can become the norm, and that is "Do What Is Right". This can only come from ridding ourselves of fear and responding only with love. But how do we change fear into love?

**Changing FEAR Into LOVE in 9 Simple Steps**

There is no trick or magic involved in turning fear into love. It takes discipline, persistence, and perseverance. You don't need to take courses or pay for psychological sessions nor expensive hypnosis. It can be done in the comfort of your home, quietly on your breaks at work, or anytime you deem appropriate. However, to be effective, you must work on it every day. The amount of time each day depends on you and your schedule. No one can set this limit or time and space for you.

I like puzzles because I like mysteries and trying to solve them. Every problem, in my estimation, has a solution. It just takes a bit of creativity, another favorite of mine. The solution to the puzzle is already there. You just have to give yourself time to put the pieces together.

In some of the puzzle books, there is what is called a "changeling challenge" whereby you are presented the task of changing a word with a given amount of letters into another word with the same amount of letters in a given number of steps. Sometimes the person completing the challenge can complete it in an even less number of steps; sometimes it might take the challenger a greater number of steps. For example, you may be asked to change the word GRAFT into TRAIN in 5 steps. Mind you, you can change only one letter at a time. It would probably look like this, keeping in mind that there are other solution possibilities:

|  | G R A F T |  | T R A I N |
|---|---|---|---|
| *(Step 1)* | G R A N T |  | B R A I N |
| *(Step 5)* |  |  |  |
| *(Step 2)* | G R A N D | B R A N D | B R A I D |
| *(Step 4)* |  |  |  |

## (Step 3)

As you can see, we changed:

*"F" to "N" in Step 1*
*Then "G" to "B" in Step 2*
*Then "N" to "I" in Step 3*
*Then "D" to "N" in Step 4*
*Finally, "B" to "T" in Step 5*

GRAFT, which means, when used as a verb denotatively – to implant or transplant from one thing to another. This could imply that one part is being overtaken by another, or as in surgery, when tissue is grafted (attached to) or put into another, meaning the original is changed, and in some cases, no longer valid.

It can also mean connotatively as a noun – a form of political corruption defined as the unscrupulous use of a politician's authority for personal gain. TRAIN which means, when used as a verb denotatively – to develop or form the habits, thoughts, or behavior of (a child or other person) by discipline and instruction; or to make proficient by instruction and practice, as in some art, profession, or work. It can also mean as a noun – a line or procession of persons, vehicles, animals, etc., traveling together.

In performing this process, you have changed

something geared toward selfish motives (GRAFT) to that which benefits everyone and even connects others in the process (TRAIN).

Keep in mind that the words can have a different connotative meaning in your own life based on your own experiences, knowledge, and frame of reference. In either case, in 5 steps you have changed the literal and more importantly, the connotative meaning in your own life. You have solved a particular challenge in your life. Notice we use the word "challenges" and not "problems".

So let's get started. Here is my given solution to changing FEAR (False Evidence Appearing Real) into LOVE (Life of Verifiable Evidence).

**Step 1: FEAR to DEAR – Change "F" to "D"**

Define what fear looks like in your life. It comes in so many shapes, sizes, and situations. It can rear its head in the form of a person, closed spaces, or activity, such as flying or driving. It can take form in social situations such as dating, marriage, having children, or rejection by peers. It can even be fear of scarcity, not having enough food, water, and shelter, which comes from the fear of not having a job or money resource. It can be fear of death, that is, for some, the great unknown. Whatever your fear looks like, you call it out and acknowledge it. You must be completely and totally honest with yourself. Sometimes our fear comes from something we didn't get to say or do and now the person involved has passed on, out of reach, or whereabouts unknown. Sometimes it's regret over something we did say or do and now feel there's no chance for forgiveness. Most of us carry these burdens which are just another form of fear.

    An important part of the process is to write down your fears. We live in a technologically advanced age today. Most of us depend so heavily on computers, cell phones, and "Alexis". In an electrical shutdown, most activity stops because most don't know what to do in their specific situation. People feel they just have to take their cell phones or chrome books everywhere they go, even to the bathroom!

    My question to those of us old enough to remember: what did you do before cell phones came along, before email came along? You waited until you got back home and called your loved ones. You also wrote them letters. This last part is the first step to turning FEAR into LOVE. "Dear _____" You fill in the blank. It might be a person or situation. Write to that fear. Tell it what issues it has caused you. Apologize to the person. Confront the person or the issue. Tell him, her, or it exactly how you feel. Don't blame the person or the issue. Take ownership of your own emotions. This removes all false pretenses. Unless it was a person or something that directly caused your physical hurt, and sometimes it is, that person or thing did not do the harm to you. You cause the harm or hurt emotion in yourself based on how you reacted to what was said or done. Remember, you can only control you, not others. What others think about you is not nearly as important as what you think and feel about yourself.

Work on this first step for how long it takes. Also, my suggestion is to write it down with pen and paper. For me, and I cannot speak for everyone, when I write, all my inner emotions seem to flow from the pen to the ink on the paper. This not only relaxes me, but my issues seem to flow onto the written page out in the open where I can examine them and resolve them. I then, at a later date, type up what I've handwritten. Then I can edit and revise as it suits me. This is my process. You must do what works best for you.

**Step 2 – Change DEAR to DEAD – Change "R" to "D"**

You've already made a major change in Step 1 by acknowledging your fears. You've written letters to either persons, living or no longer living, and issues and situations or challenges that kept you in a state of fear, depression, or anxiety. Now it's time to make the next change. It's time for you to bury those fears. When something is dead to you, you hold a funeral or memorial service. This is a different kind of funeral. Instead of sadness, it's a celebration, a celebration of your success at overcoming the fears of the person or challenges.

Set up an altar with all of the letters you've written. Candles are optional; however, it's your altar. You pick the most appropriate place. You are saying goodbye to the fears. You are celebrating your victory. Remember, you still have 7 more steps to go, but you always speak and act as if it is already done and accomplished.

**Step 3 – Change DEAD to HEAD   Change "D" to "H"**

When we think of the head, it brings to mind several aspects, such as the brain which does the thinking function in the physical body. It responds to all the impulses sent to it from the other cells. This is where the conscious mind dwells that interprets the frequency waves and emotions into images and symbols. It communicates to others these images and symbols through language. It is the head that takes in all the stimuli it receives, through the eyes, the ears, the nose, and mouth, even through the hair follicles and skin. It's during times of fear that we have to "keep our heads", to think logically and critically. Though we are feeling, breathing and living beings, our emotions can fool us, hinder us, and sometimes even destroy us. We cannot control everyone and everything around us, but we can control ourselves. This the key change to moving from debilitating ourselves with the challenges and the people that produced fear that we thought were dead to us, and at times will rear its or their "ugly heads", that we must keep ours.

  The best way to not give in to emotions that stem mostly from our fear is to STOP for a moment, WAIT, COUNT to 10 slowly, and then THINK about the letters you wrote in Step 1. Remember the victory you claimed in Step 2. Remember how good it felt to release that fear that is trying to ease back into your life. Remember to head forward. Don't react. Give yourself time and space, if possible. Believe it or not, time and space is all there really is. All else is an illusion. You are still headed in the right direction. Keep going.

**Step 4: Change HEAD to HERD – Change "A" to "R"**

  It is said that there is power in numbers. It is the

culmination of energies that brings this power, that is, that intensifies it. One buffalo is powerful, but a whole herd is even more so. Man was not meant to be alone. If this were the case, there would have been no way to procreate and there would never have existed multitude of herds. The last thing any of us should do is give into the myth and propaganda of scarcity. As long as we hold to the principles of "give and take" and keep ourselves open to sharing and caring, there is and will always be enough for everyone.

That is why the next step to changing fear into love is to remember the herd. We need all of those around us. We really do need each other. Stop allowing differences, whether they be ethnic background, skin color, hair texture, eye shape and color, hair color, physical shape and frame, religious belief, political affiliation, education level, social status, or the like, to separate and divide us from the herd. We are individual entities with our own special traits, qualities, gifts, talents, ideas and creativity. Let's always cherish these and use them to benefit the herd, which is mankind. We don't have to *compete* against the herd; we just need to *complete* the herd. We are all a part of each other. It is man who draws lines of division, whether these lines are relational, political, social, or geographical. It is fear that makes men do so. A herd mentality can erase these lines and at the same time erase all the fears that come with them.

## Step 5: Change HERD to HERE – Change "D" to "E"

Often when we are told to move forward, we are told to just put one foot in front of the other and keep walking. However, this is easier said than done. So much of our time is wasted over past mistakes, past regrets, and past failures, that we allow the fear of repeating them inhibit our ability to move forward. Sometimes it is the fear of the unknown that stagnates us. In reality, there is no such thing as past and future when it relates to time. In reality, there is only the present time.

This leads to the next step to make changes to go from fear to love. Practice living in the present, that is, practice being "here". It is like exercising a muscle. Yesterday and tomorrow are illusions. Though beautiful to sing, leave "Yesterday" to the Beatles and "Tomorrow" to Little Orphan Annie. There is really only now, today, this moment. If we can train our minds to remember this and do one simple thing, and that is to focus. Say "I am HERE". I love. I breath. I think. I exist right now. Take yourself away from TV, movies, magazines, books, cell phones, and computers for at least an hour each day. The optimal time to spend away from such distractions is 3 hours each day for those with families, 2 hours each day for those with jobs, 1 hour for those with their own businesses, and 4 hours for those who have none of the above. Some will say this is not possible to do. Nothing is impossible. We are the ones who put limits and time constraints on ourselves. We fear we'll lose our jobs (future), we fear our businesses will go under (future), we fear we'll lose our friends and family (future). Most of our time is spent fearing our past mistakes and what will happen in the future. They are all illusions!

Here's a test to prove it. Take a long deep breath, hold it for the count of 5, then let out the breath very slowly. That breath is life. It fuels the blood so that the heart can beat and pump blood through your veins and arteries. Each heartbeat represents the moments in your life. You cannot get back any of the ones gone before. Each new and present moment is a gift, a miracle from your Creator, the Great Consciousness. It is important to take time to treasure each moment you can, and realize just how precious you are. No matter what hardships or trials you've been through, you've weathered each storm. You've conquered every trial. How do I know? Because you're alive right now, reading these words. Rejoice, my friend, and remember *YOU ARE HERE!*

**Step 6: HERE to HARE – Change "E" to "A"**

Most of us know the story of the Tortoise and the Hare. The way the story goes is that these two animals were having a race. The tortoise, we all know of course, is a slow moving creature. The hare is swift and runs fast. The goal of the race was to make it to the finish line first. The hare started off quickly but he moved so fast that he eventually "ran out of gas" and couldn't make it to the finish line. So, the tortoise who kept his same steady and slow pace was able to finish and win the race and therefore "beat" the hare. This children's story is told to illustrate a moral that the race is not given to the swift, but to the strong, that is, to those who can endure to the end. Sounds great, however, once again, we see how the competitive spirit is instilled in us early in life.

Be that as it may, this leads us to the next step to changing fear into love. Remember the hare and learn from him. His fear was that the tortoise would reach the goal before him. He felt he had to compete against another creature. He felt he had to prove he was the "best". Of course, he felt he had to show he was the fastest. His ego, vanity, and pride were all factors.

The reality is that the only one the hare had to really compete against was himself. He only needed to be the best he could be. In other words, instead of focusing on someone else, he needed to develop his own strengths, work on his own weaknesses, and use his gifts and talents to reach his goal. He would have been better off recognizing the qualities of the tortoise and being grateful there are steady and slow creatures that exist. Like the hare, the tortoise exists for a purpose. We waste time putting down others and trying to find a way to make ourselves seem so much more than someone else. If your gift is speed like the hare, use it to better yourself, to help others who are not as fast, and work together so that we all reach the "finish line" together.

**Step 7: Change HARE to LARE – Change "H" to "L"**

The next step to changing fear to love is to focus on and pinpoint that which we "lare" in our lives. In other words, that fear that we "feed" or "fatten". These are the things that trap you and are trigger points that ensnare you and lure you back into your specific fears. These are those cherished possessions of fear of which you are unaware. Not everyone has the same fears. For some it is jealousy and envy, which leads to anger and resentment, and can lead to committing crimes such as theft, assault and even murder. Sometimes this "murder" can be through the death of important relationships through the words we speak. It is not always easy to see that the cause was fear. However, it usually stems from fear of loss, fear of abandonment, fear of no longer having the affections of another, or fear of losing the presumed affections and fame from others who previously commented on how good they thought you were at your achievements, or even fear of not getting many likes on your social media projects or videos.

What we "lare" (feed or fatten) are sometimes those traps or fears of which we may be consciously unaware. These are the most dangerous. It takes quiet meditation and introspection each day to reveal and pinpoint them. It is a good idea to start a journal, if you don't already have one. Successful people write things down. Each day, try to pinpoint a specific moment or event when you felt pangs of fear. Remember, the fear could be in any shape or form. Think about what your reaction was. Remember what thoughts ran through your mind and the words you spoke, if you did speak anything at the time. Thoughts always come first, then actions.

We are not advocating not protecting yourselves when there is real danger or threat to your life or to your family and loved ones. The natural response to real danger is fight or flight. Just make sure it is real and not an illusion. Most of the time we are fighting or running from our own fear that brought on the illusion of a threat.

For example, there was a story told by motivational speaker, Les Brown, of a friend of his who, as a boy, was terrorized every day by a neighborhood dog who saw him coming and would start to bark ferociously and then chase him down the street. This went on for weeks until the boy decided he'd had enough. He decided that he was no longer going to run from this dog. This time, when the dog barked and ran up to him, he stood his ground and didn't run away. To his amazement, he discovered that the dog literally had no teeth! Much like most of our fears.

Our minds are powerful. It is up to us to control our thoughts and our behaviors. There is always a reaction to what we do and say, and many times consequences as well. It is up to us to pinpoint and isolate the traps and triggers brought on by our fears and what we lare (feed or fatten). When they rear their ugly heads, just remember that the "bark" is usually worse than the "bite".

### Step 8: Change LARE to LORE – Change "A" to "O"

When we think of lore, the word "folklore" comes to mind. These are the stories we tell based on our heritage, culture, roots, and customs. Most of the time they contain legends and myths handed down to us from our ancestors. Grandparents love telling these stories to their grandchildren. However, the lore we want should be based on truth of who we are.

This brings us to the next step to changing fear into love. Knowing our true selves, knowing our identity, our heritage, our roots, our language and culture. Do you really know who you are or do you merely go by some label stamped upon you, some category cast upon you, or some caste system you are told in which you fit and must stay?

Knowing your roots and heritage starts with research. Jotting down all that you think you know as a starting point. Going through family records and albums given to you by your parents, grandparents, aunts, uncles, and cousins. Then, talking with family members to gain more information from them. Then getting records and information from your church/ mosque/ temple/parish or the like. Getting records from schools, military, social clubs and organizations. Searching newspapers and archives can give valuable information also. Building a family tree can be a long and arduous tasks, but it can also be very rewarding. Most people even get DNA tests; however, they can be limiting and sometimes very inaccurate.

The manner and type of research you use is entirely up to you. Remember, this lore is just your starting point. These are your roots. These are the stories that once defined your beginnings. They should be cherished and told if you wish, but the real goal is to now start writing your own stories. It is your time to create a new lore. What do you want the world, your heirs, your family and friends to remember about you and your life? What footprint do you want to leave?

When you visit the cemeteries or read about those who have passed on, it is the date (usually just the year) they were born, then a dash ("-") followed by the date (or year) they died. Unless you knew the person or delve into their life history, works, family, and achievements, you would never know what the little dash represents. That dash is their "lore". It is the many stories that represent their life. It encompasses all their hopes, dreams, loves, and yes, even the fears they had. They no longer exist in that same shape and form. They no longer occupy that same space and time.

We say they have "died" but their stories, their lore, lives on. Whether good, bad, or indifferent to others, they existed. Their footprint is etched in time and that little dash speak volumes.

Those of us who know better, understand that matter is neither created nor destroyed. It changes but still exists. No matter if you call it the soul, the spirit, the ether, frequency, electromagnetic waves, or ghost, that part of each being, that essence of who you are, is eternal and lives on. You are a part of the Great Consciousness. As the cycle goes – it dissipates out, breaks itself apart to experience life and existence in different shapes and forms – then brings itself together again as a whole. When you realize this, you can be free to "write" your lore at this point in time, totally without fear.

When you realize you don't actually die, there is no fear. We fear the unknown. However, where would be the mystery, the intrigue, all the enjoyment of discovery if you always knew everything beforehand? Think how boring life would be. Think about the time you've started on a new adventure, moved to a new area, fell in love and started a new relationship. Remember the excitement and anticipation of what would come? Think about a mystery you had been reading or a movie you were anticipating watching and someone told you "the butler did it". Remember how disappointed you were that they ruined the ending for you. Life goes on, so does the mystery and discovery. Count it all joy!

You realize that you're learning to trust, not just yourself but the Great Consciousness. You have never, ever, been alone in any trial, trouble, situation or catastrophe. There is nothing that happens to you, whether we consider it a tragedy, comedy, or drama, that the real you has not or cannot survive. Our bodies, these houses, are temporary. You take care of it, nourish it, and nurture it to make it last as long as possible. If you wish, technology has evolved such that you can take advantage of cloning or other means so you can stay here longer. To each his or her own. Personally, I'm looking forward to what the Great Consciousness has in store for me. I'm going to establish my lore at this point in time, in this house gifted to me. When I am done, I'll move on to the next stage without fear. You and I have a new and exciting lore to write.

**Step 9:  Change LORE to LOVE – Change "R" to "V"**

They say perfect love casts out all fear. This brings us to the last step to changing fear into love. From Step 1 to

Step 8, we have been working on our individual changes. We have been attempting to perfect ourselves, that is, become the best that we can be. No competition with others. We cannot change others, as stated before, only ourselves. What we can do out of the love we have for ourselves and others is to share with them. We can do this through a method that doesn't cost one red cent. It's the act of love that I, the author, have been doing throughout this book: communicating. I have been sharing my fears, my discoveries, my gifts, my knowledge and wisdom, and the knowledge and wisdom of those whom I have researched, with my readers.

Communication can come through different ways. It does not always have to be words. There is non-verbal communication through gestures or touch, through sounds such as music, and through actions by a smile or baking a cake for a loved one, or visiting an elderly person in a convalescent home, or holding a baby or child who has been abandoned, or a simple prayer when someone needs it the most. Perhaps you are a writer, a poet, or a musician. You can take everything you've done in Steps 1 through 9 and share it through your particular gift, maybe even through painting, sculpture, pottery, or dance. Whatever the means, you are free to love. You have completely changed fear into love. You can share this love with another person. You've finally discovered that all it took was making simple changes one step at a time, and that all you really had to fear was fear itself. You've changed all the False Evidence Appearing Real (FEAR) into a Life Of Verifiable Evidence (LOVE).

These are the changes you've made:

**F  H  R  E  A  L  O  V**

It is with your own creativity that you can now rearrange your life, just as we can rearrange these letters to spell:

**H  A  L  F  O  V  E  R**

Half the battle is over, that is, the losing part is over. You are now free to win. This is your moment in time as Whitney Houston sang so eloquently. Now make it shine!

## Conclusion

*Love is a fabric which never fades, no matter how often it is washed in the water of adversity and grief.*
*- Robert Fulghum -*

Once we know and operate in love, there is no longer a need to compete. Once we remove the debilitating and destructive monetary system and replace it with contributionism, there is no longer the need to compete whereby we have to destroy everything and everyone around us to become "No. 1". We can play games, sports, etc. for fun and enjoy it. Even if we do want to keep score, it will be reduced to mere "Okay, but I'll get you next time" and meant only playfully from the heart of the little child that still lives within us. Our daily survival does not depend on it. Our sense of self-worth does not depend on it. Our relationships and families well-being does not depend on it. Our progress and evolution as creative thinking human beings does not depend on it. We can finally realize those words written on parchment but inscribed forever in our hearts: *"life, liberty, and the pursuit of happiness"*.

www.ingramcontent.com/pod-product-compliance
Lightning Source LLC
Chambersburg PA
CBHW070448050426
42451CB00015B/3390